High Shelf

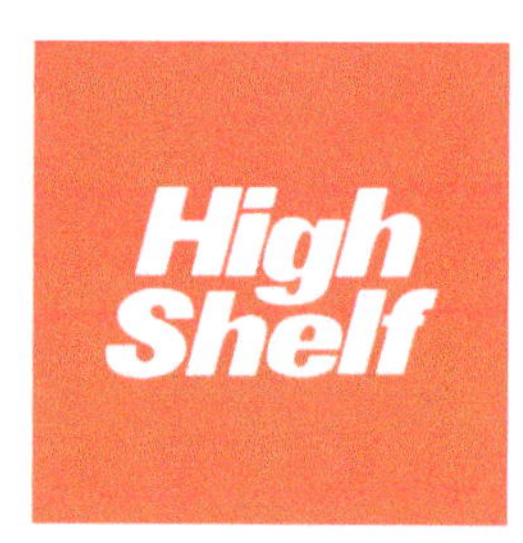

High Shelf Issue XIX. June 2020.
Portland, Oregon.
Copyright 2020, High Shelf Press

ISBN: 978-1-952869-99-0

Cover Image by Raman Bhardwaj
Design and Layout by C. M. Tollefson
Edited by David Seung & C. M. Tollefson
With Special Thanks to River Elizabeth Hall & Kristin Howe

High Shelf XIX

June 2020

"... What is hidden in this continent?
Where I cannot see, hear,
nor breathe, nor move.
No return.
It is not very different than the thought of it... "
Leon Fedolfi

"... I am sailor who cannot find land,
        alone
                in his vessel upon the sea

My body is ethereal foam
            and my soul, homeless wind..."
Felipe Echeverría

Table Of Contents

Stay Home

Aidan White

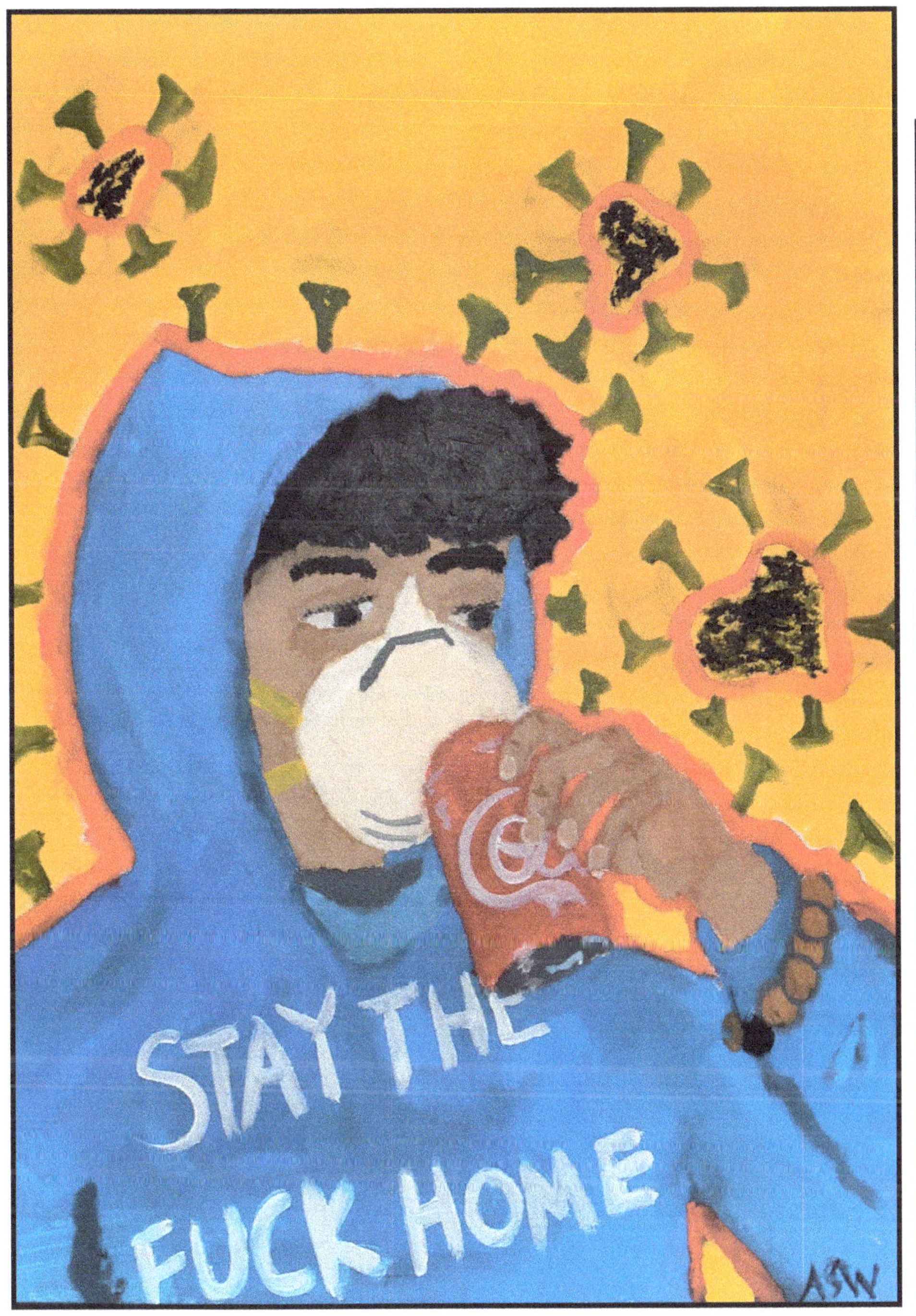

edges

Peter Engen

am I enough
to carry our monsters from
the pillow to the burn pile where

there's a stump by the red barn that
was used to butcher chickens but
we don't do that anymore because you
started cutting yourself below the knee with
a thin blade from a broken pencil sharpener and

it looked like a rake of slow paper cuts when
you lifted your pant leg at the clinic while
the doctor spoke like a metronome about
gathering things with sharp edges into a safe
place until it felt like a screaming teakettle left
too long on the stove and I

kept asking the invisible if I
am strong enough to be the bear skin you need me to be
am I thick enough to hold it all together and
wrap myself fully around our hungry fears as
the long grey face of winter pushes
against the windows when

you know
that I know
that we know
why there's a pause between
saying "I love you sweetheart" and "goodnight" now
leaving our bedroom doors open just a bit to
let a handful of light from the hallway plunge
into our shadows connecting
my bed to
yours

No longer beauty

Ishani Synghal

To love the flares of your elders and be proud that
they echo in your reflection.[1]

---

[1] You saw me white light and light white, brighter than shame. You thought
my birth would change your pigment saying: *this, this is my beauty* as if you
had never been proud of anything that was yours. But I grew and the moon-
light white of your blood and tradition, the paleness you adored, was over-
shadowed. You forgot that sunlight bleaches objects but darkens human flesh
so I wore 90 SPF and Fair and Lovely Beauty Cream. Then, recoiling at your
likeness, you turned away from me. In your wake, a winter storm of bitter ice
between us, and all you said was: *december suits you*

Helsingborg & High Water

Cierra Lowe

My ancestors went blind drinking
from radiators & distilling their furniture.
Their gifts smell of ether
& iron. Their blessings
turn & rust.

My Punnett square is chain-linked. My affliction
is a family heirloom that looked garish
in every room. With left hands & blue eyes,
I have learned of recession.

I have wondered how long it would take
to distill my bedroom sets. I have wondered
how many stones my heart weighs, how
much of me was carbon. I have wondered
of my dog, now blind and in Lismore, and if he
remembers me still.

My bones are Belfast, my lungs are Dresden.
My tongue is Glasgow, my eyes are
Birkenau. Trauma is a lineage that
does not disinherit. Relief
was a coffin ship that never
made it to port.

I have prayed for hands big enough
to float me across the North Sea. I have prayed
for fealty, lucidity, sanctum. I have prayed
for vertebrae like braille that read
"have mercy."

The Silver City sleeps tonight,
still across the Atlantic—but mercy,
as it were, has been
granted.

The Characters in a Tarot Card

Katie Hogan

The hounds peel open their jaws in the foothills;
These drought-fissured Badlands teeming
With veins.   They smell the blood. Dig up the bones.
Munch on burial ground as though cremation

Could circle through their throats like communion wine.
This desert is an age-wisened womb that breeds
Mountains like Earth-staked monuments beneath
The wrong face in the sun: Crescent body smudging

Shadow across its cheeks like smoke damage.
The city that broke the wall. The two pillars
Left to plot the dust like gravel. Left like gates.
Opening to ground   where Something might grow;

The underside of the moon propped
Up like a baby's spine:

spitting up its roots.

Maya and Myth

Raman Bhardwaj

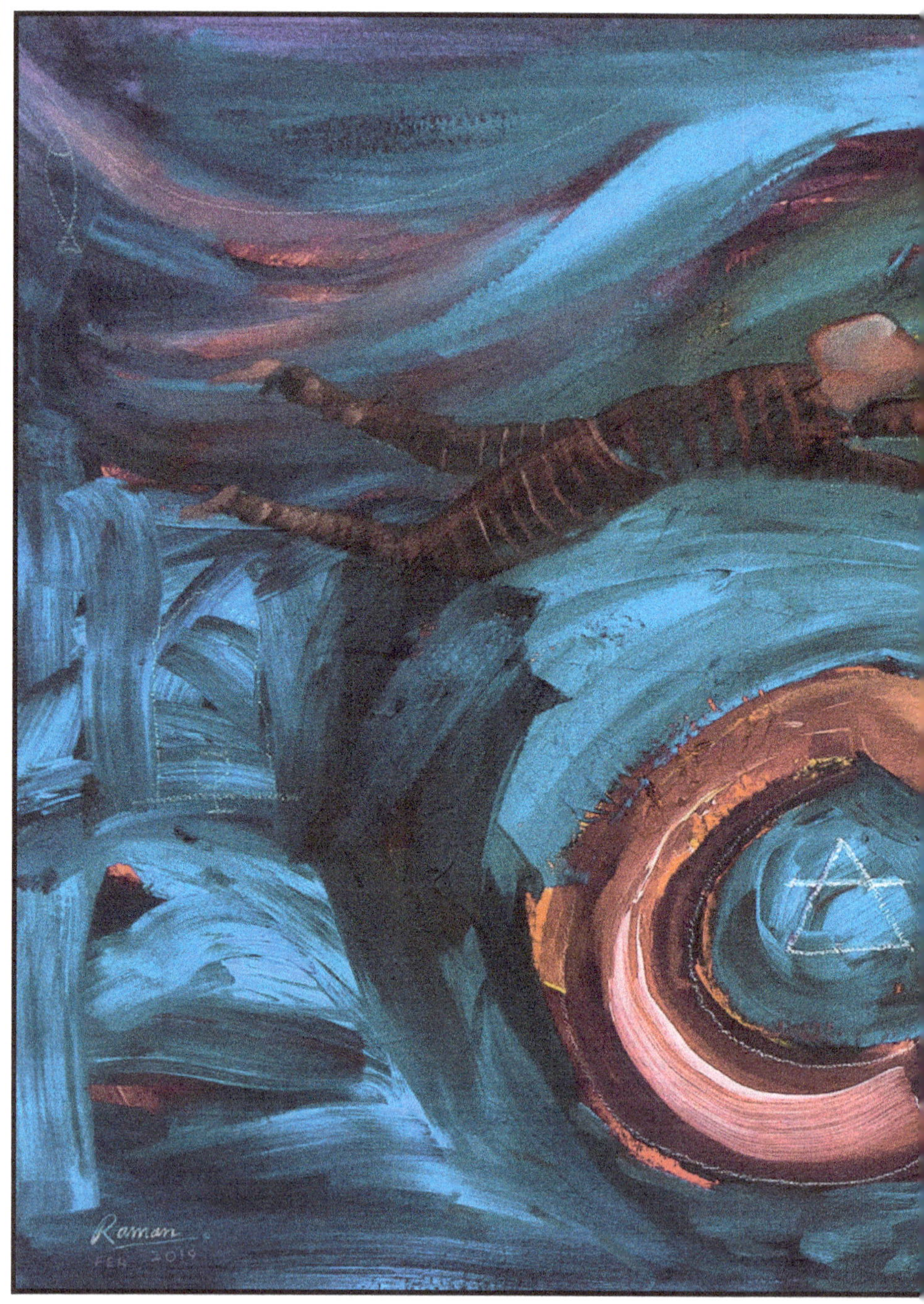

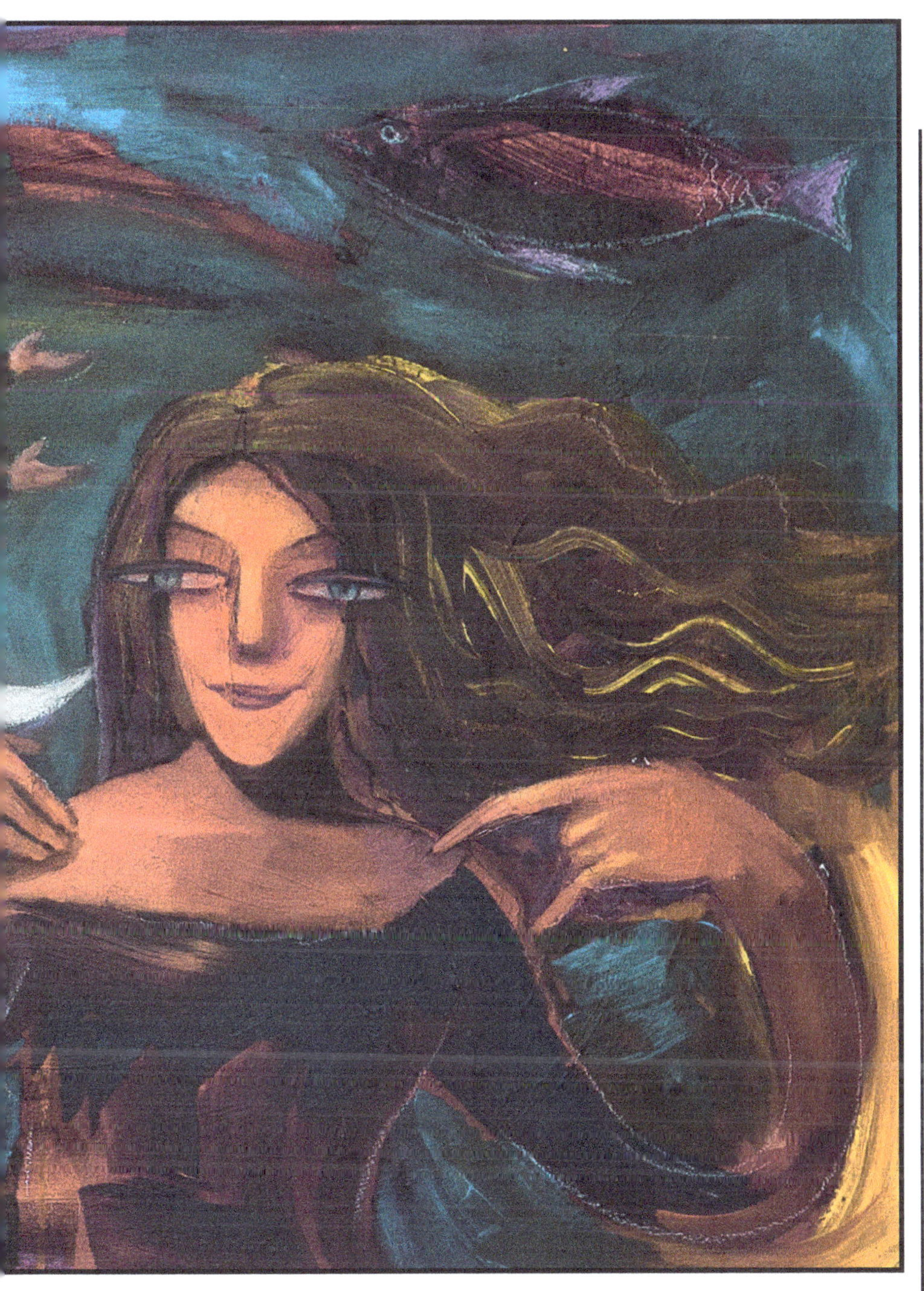

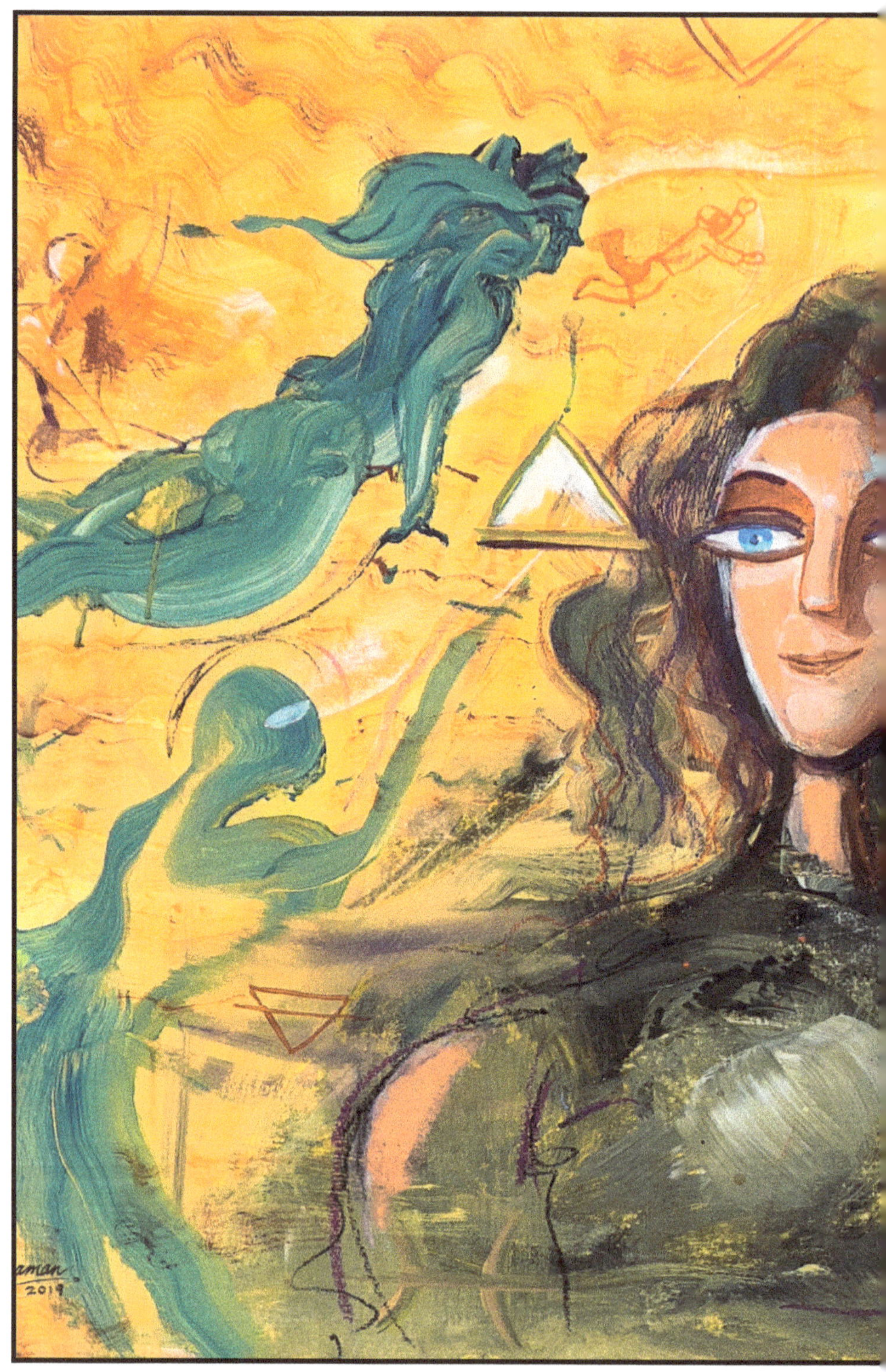

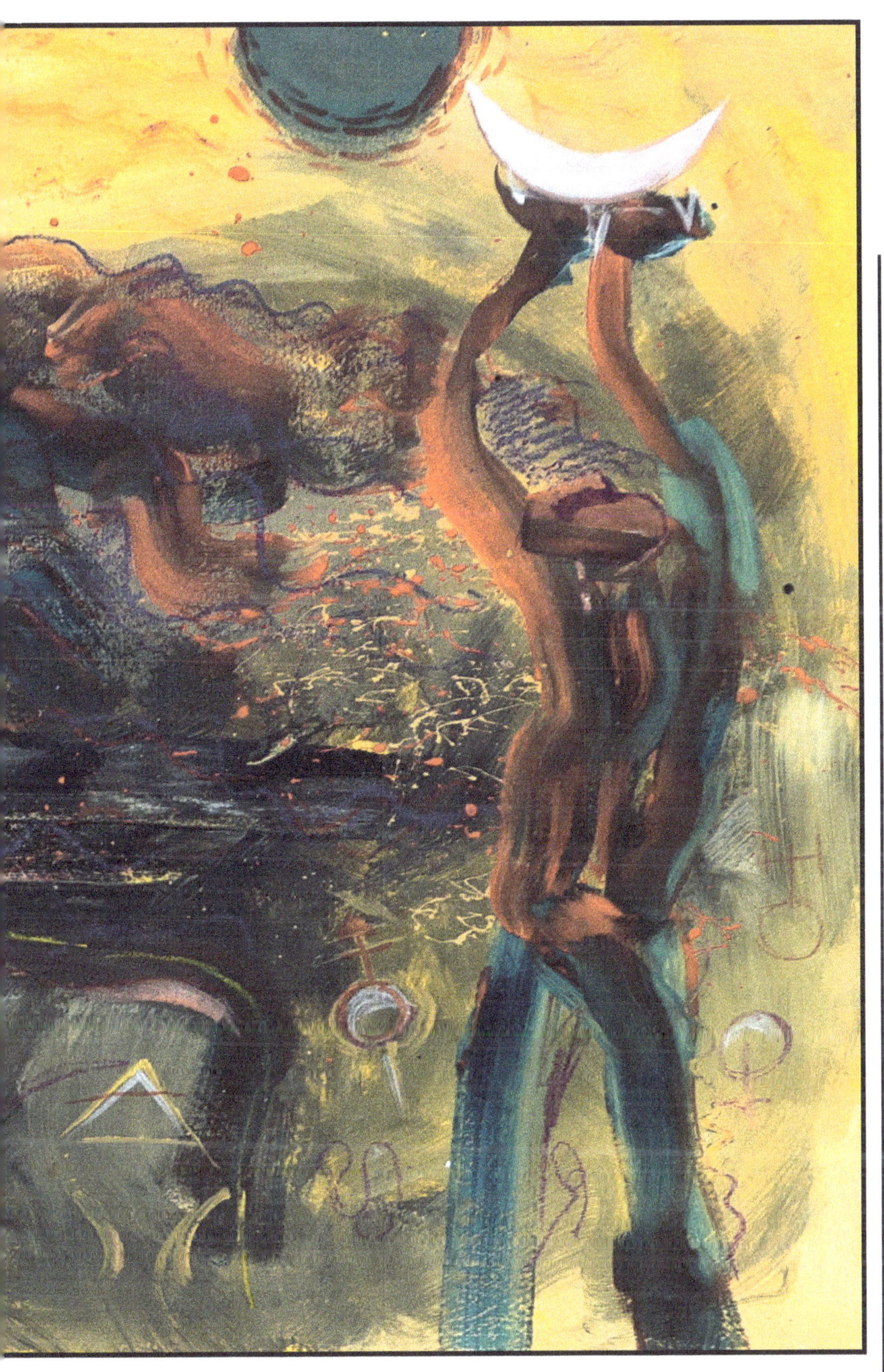

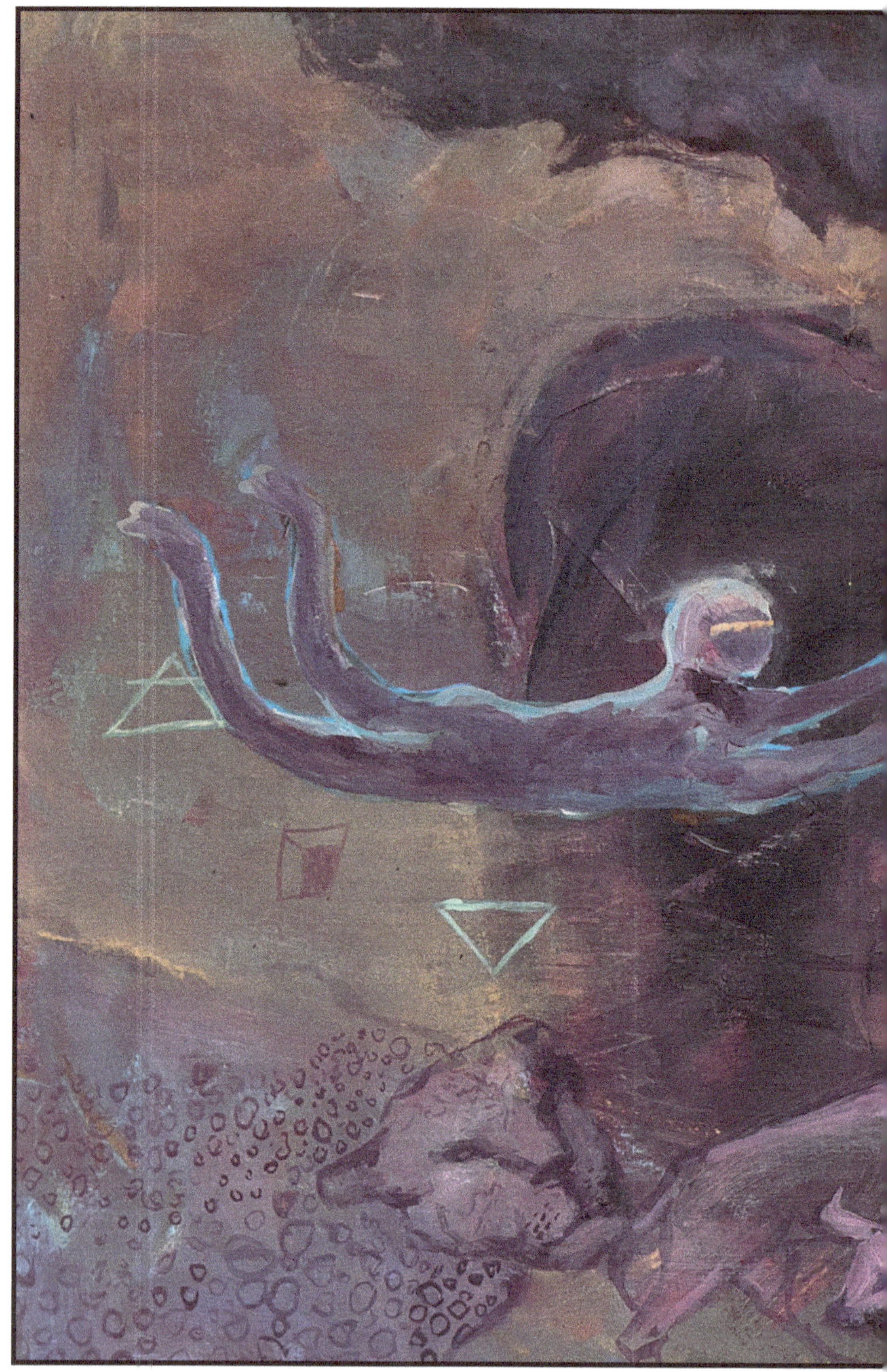

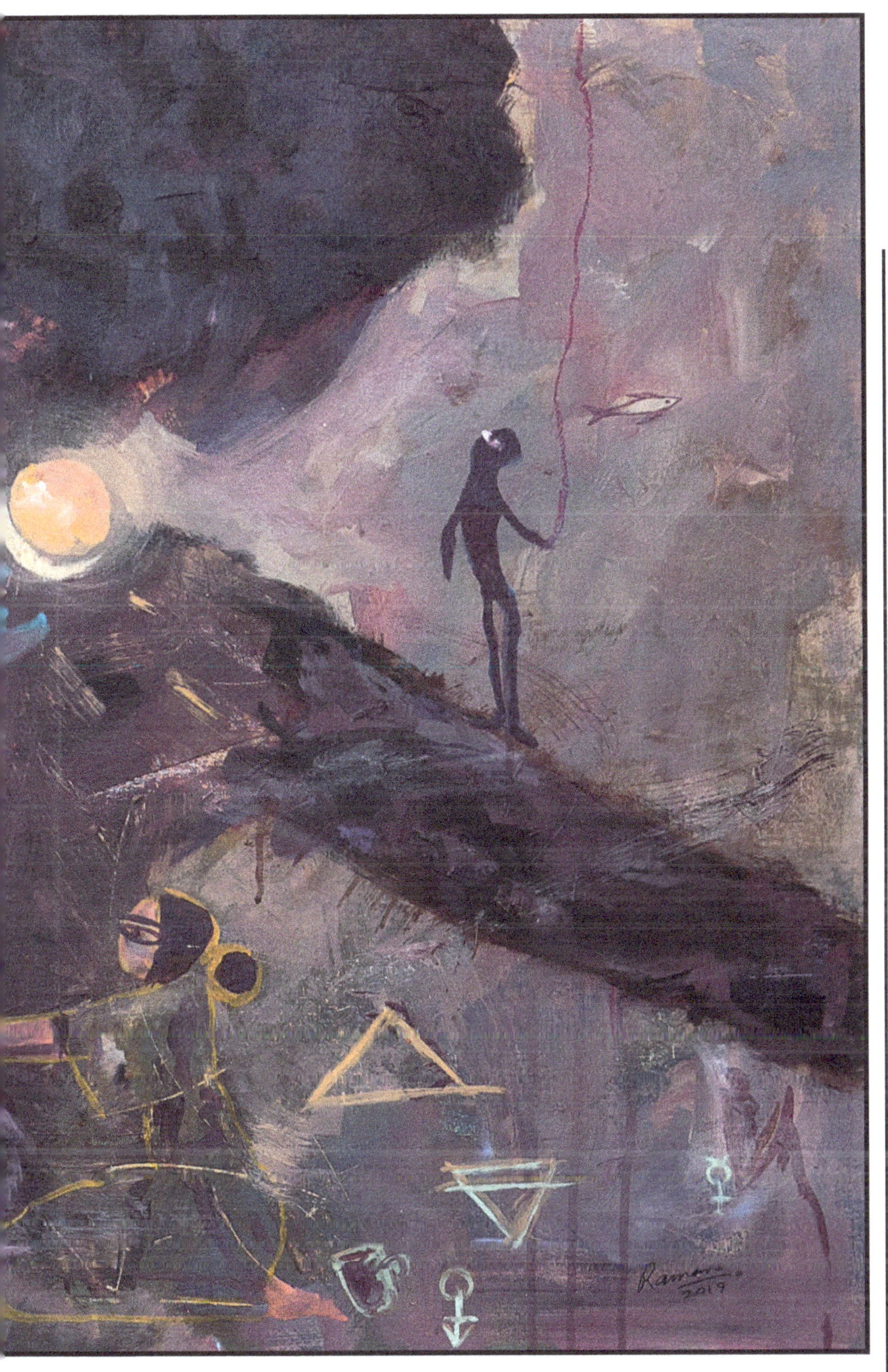

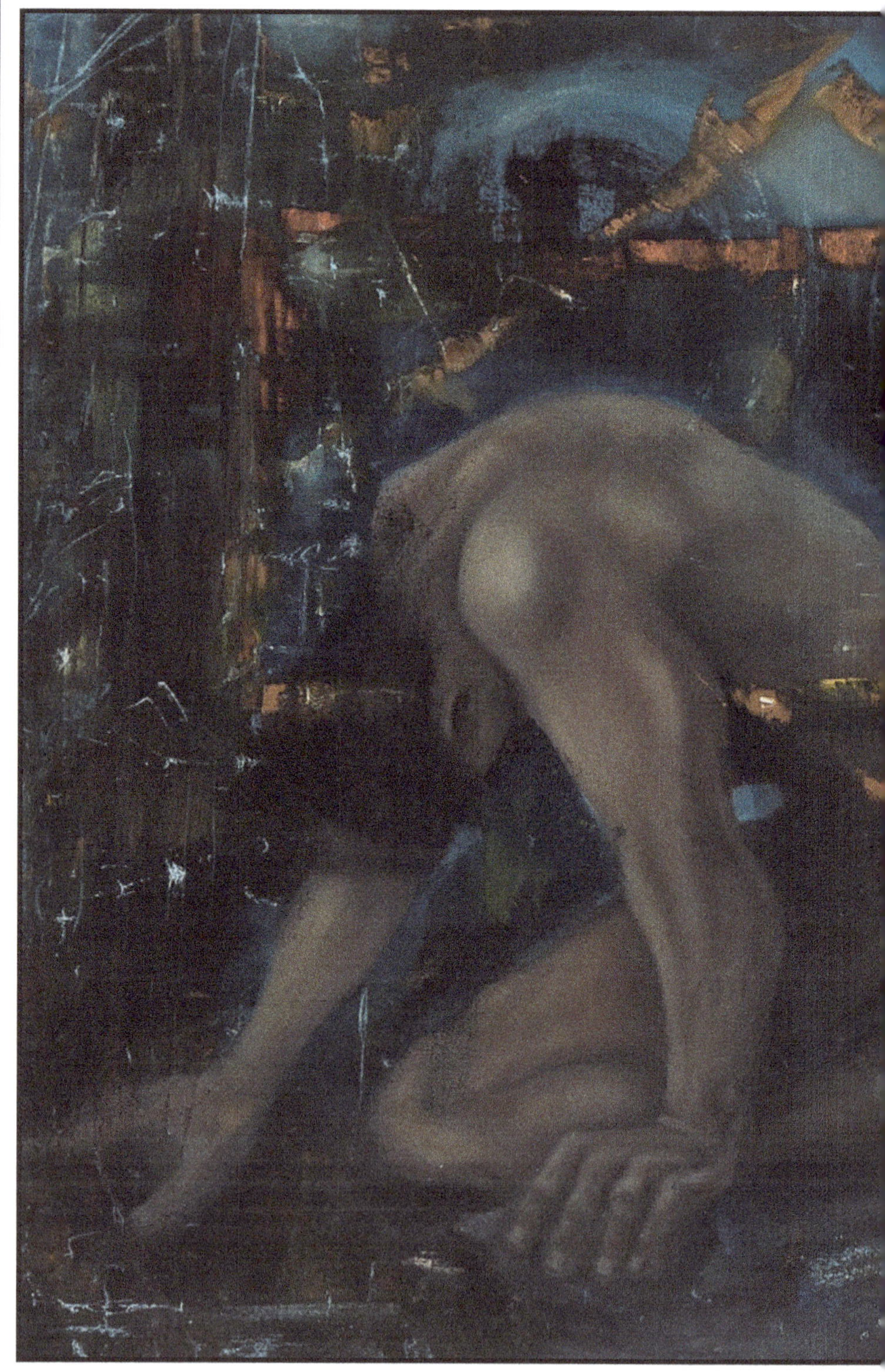

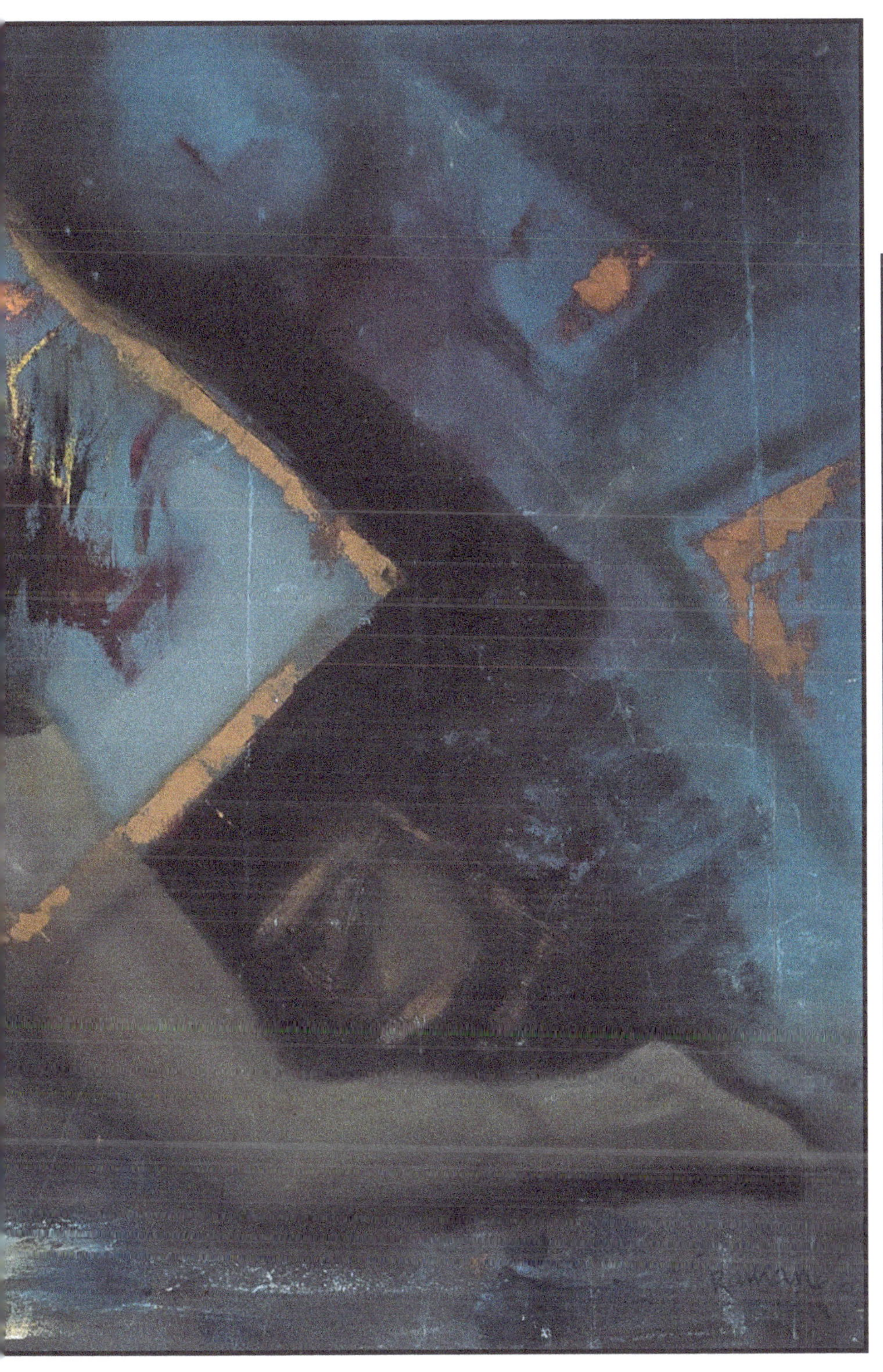

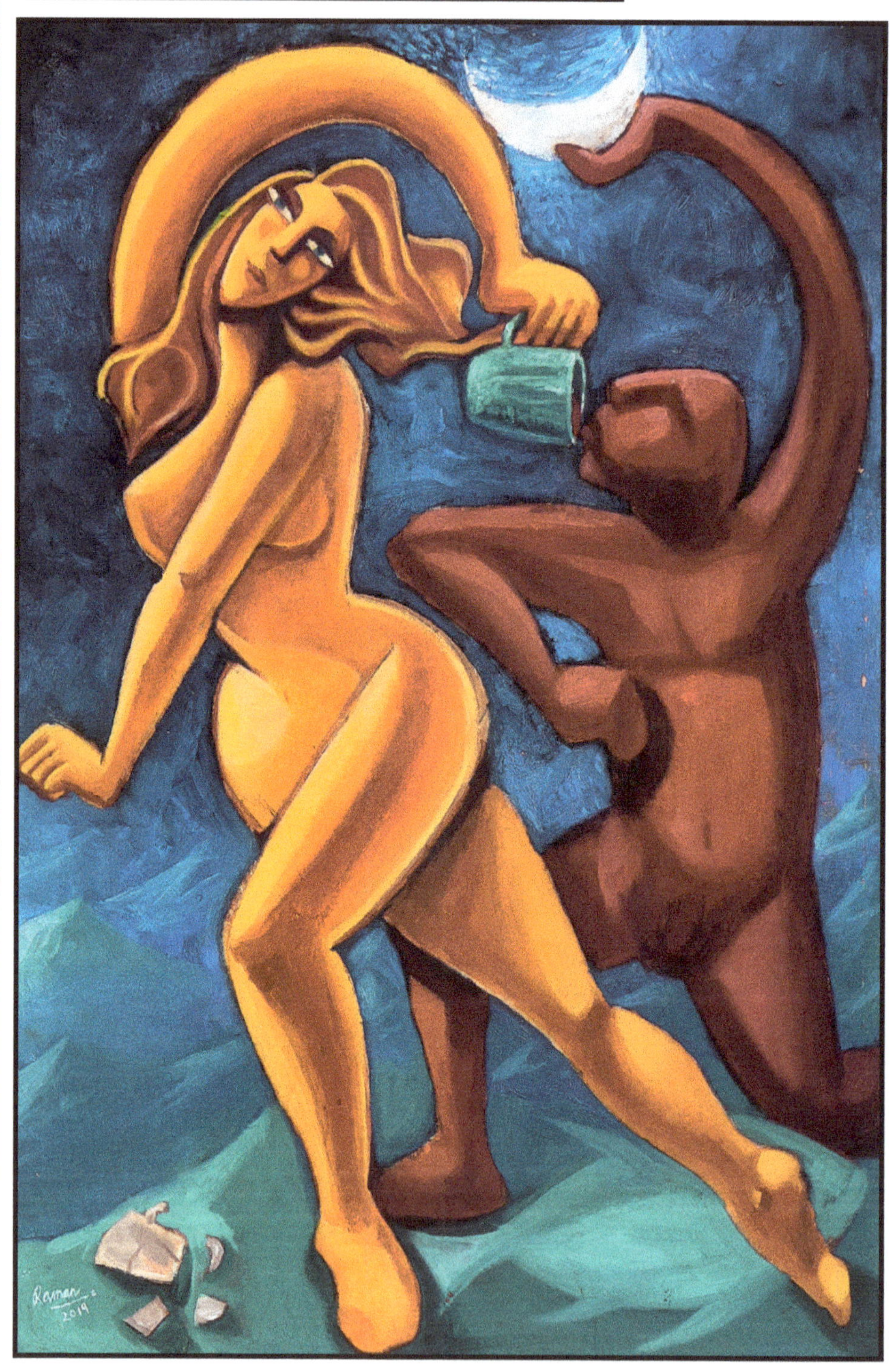

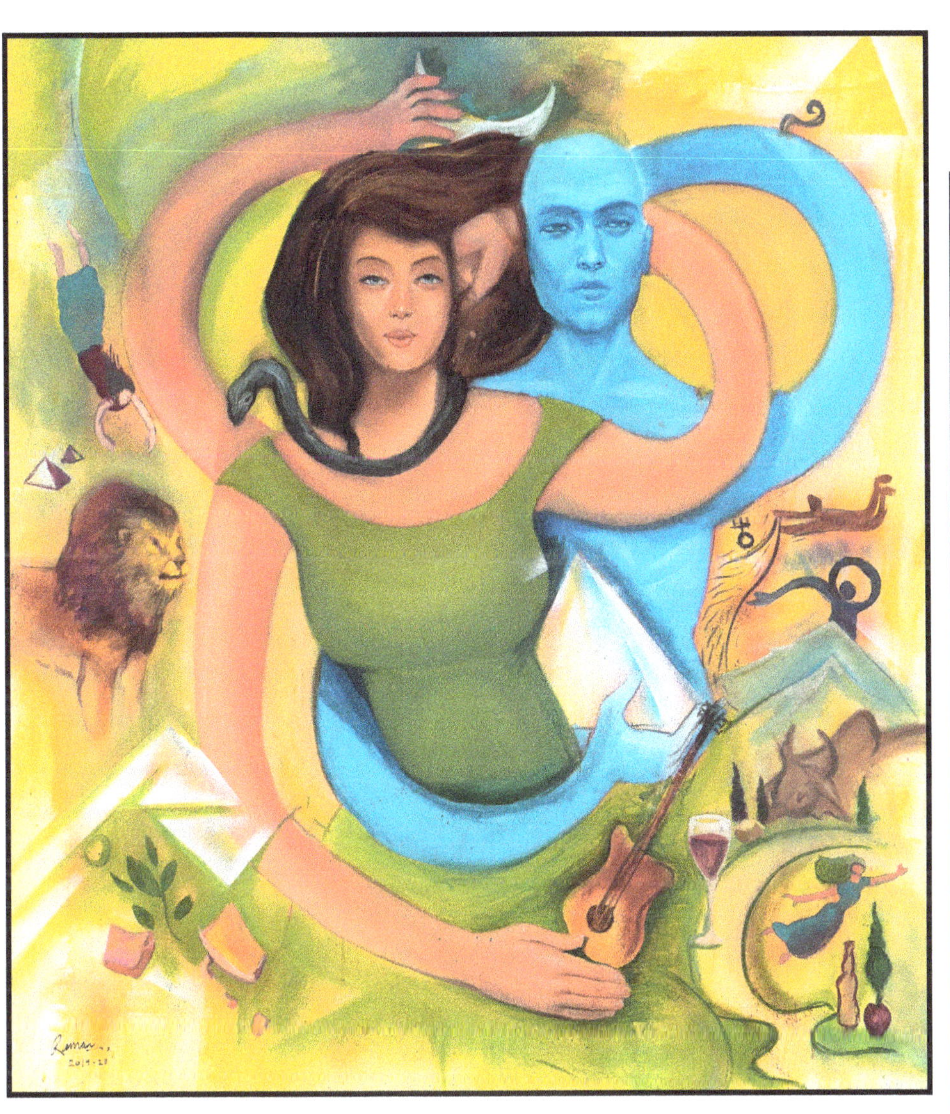

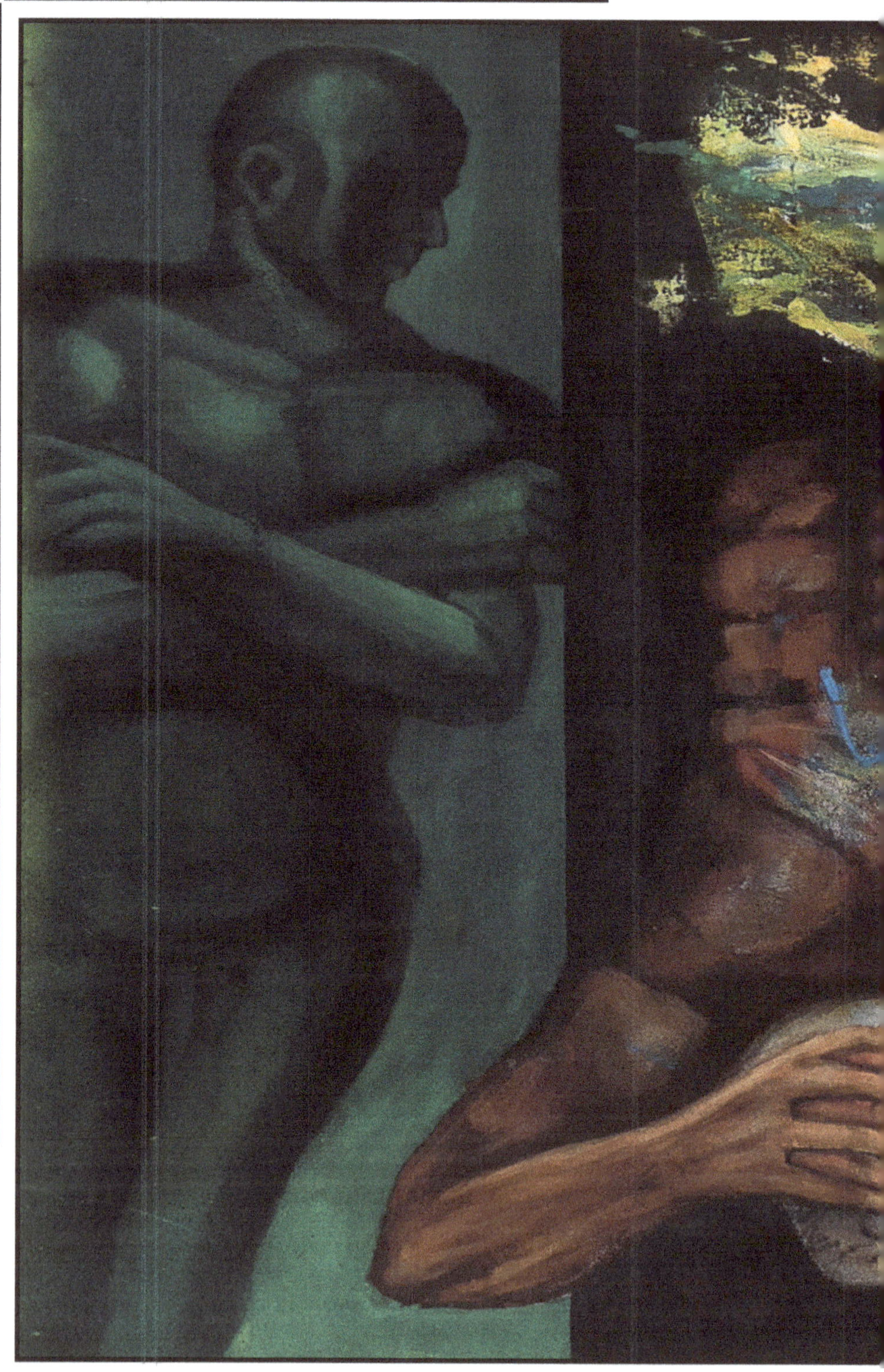

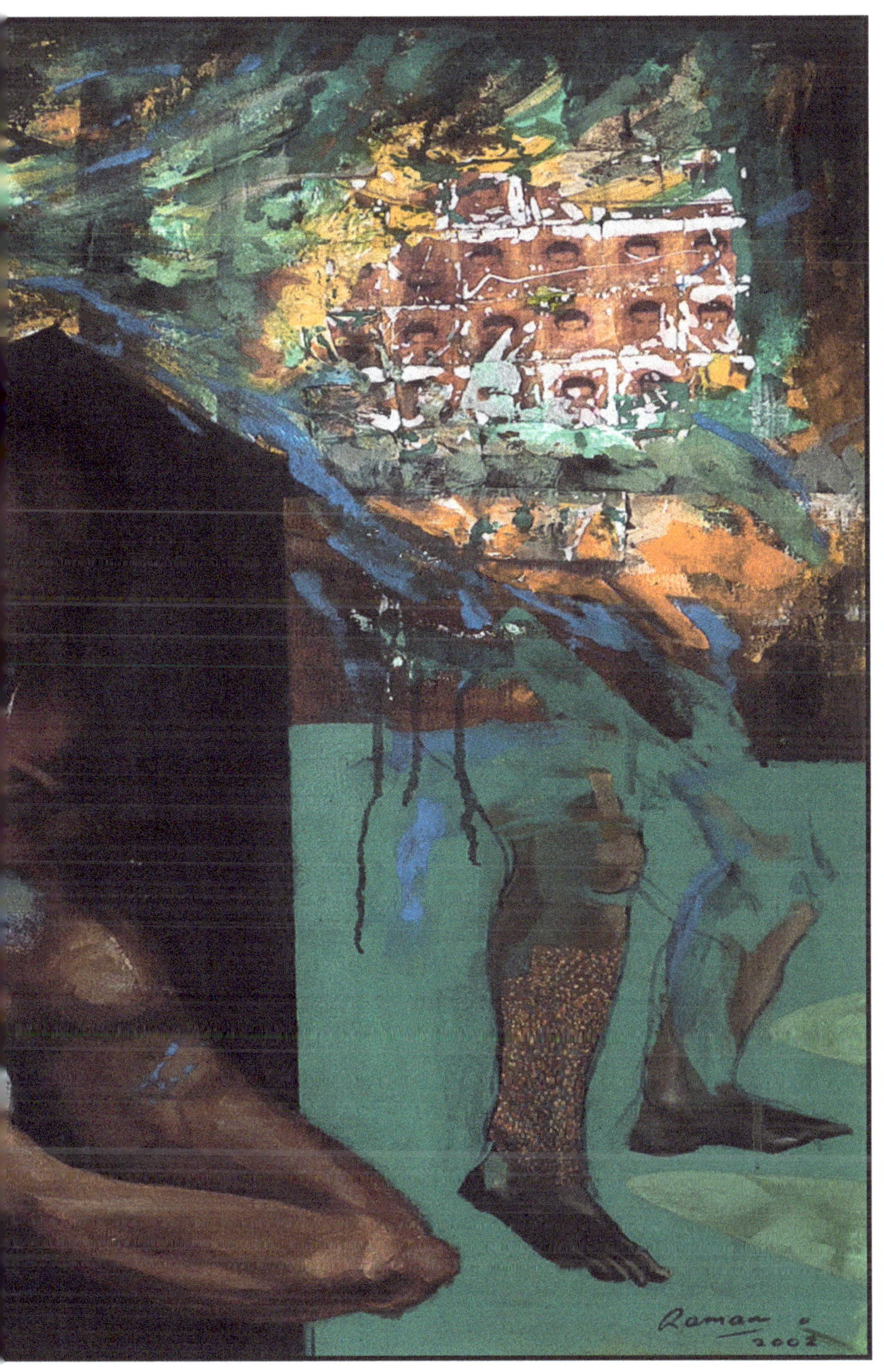

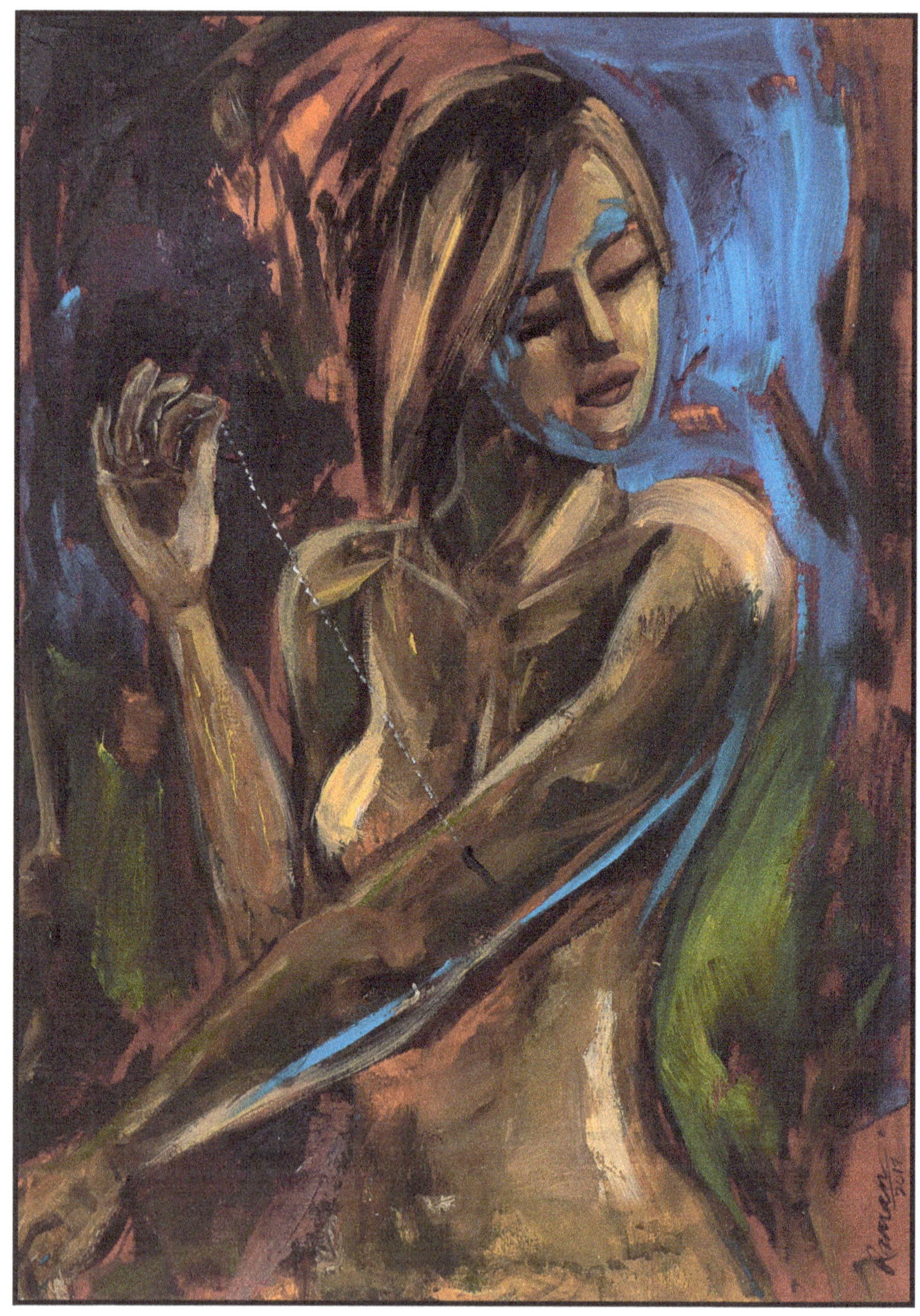

Escapism in a Motel Pool, Circa 1977.

Sophie Hoss

It's a weightless delirium.

Splayed atop the water in a back float,

the sluggish neon current stirs your hair, rings in

your ears.

Evaporating chemicals simmer low.

The chipped duplex stacked above

Is hazed in blue

and those sleazy bulbs in the *VACANCY* sign

blink in

stutters.

Dip underneath—

you take ages to sink.

When your foot

finally

Meets concrete,

you balance

on

a

single

toe,

wonder if this

is what it's like

to be a

ghost.

A water-logged fly meanders   past.

Propel yourself back upward, spring-boarding from the

bottom.

The night air is colder than it was before;

You shudder as your head breaks the surface,

as your hands grip the faux-granite ledge.

Acrid chlorine dribbles down your lip.

The last nickel of pocket change is gone—

spent on that useless phone call—and

tomorrow, you'll have to hitchhike.

Anyone's guess how long till the coast.

Ode To Vomit

Jasmine Ledesma

My mother is afraid
of fat and break-ins.
She thinks they are
the same thing.
I am ten and scared
of fire and vampires
in that order.
My reflection greases
along car windows like
smears of blood.
I steal my brother's mirror
and spend decades
looking at the girl in there.
She looks like a cloud,
moody and formed.
The first time I make myself
throw up my room is grey
with afternoon. My head
full of unfinished dopamine,
I chase my first impulse and
crawl into my throat.
Everything comes up like surprise.

Mold On Careful String

Haolun Xu

[I start to jog again, to lose weight]

I'm *lying*, again, I'm running away from the truth
as if it were easier to cast cheap hexes
like gelatin in food–

[A great wind breaks across the night sky. The moon glows, painfully.]

At night, be careful running.
You'll notice that one out of every forty trees creak loudly in the wind.

Take note that they are made from plastic and rubber,
like a person or a tumor– the electricity hums quietly but sharply
inside of this.

What is 'contamination?' This questions begs also the answer
of how to understand insulation. Is this safety,
or the absurd, like theory, being trapped in a body.

Do not approach them. Imposters,
are quite eager. If you were to strike one,
prepare to know
the jolts of a betrayed yell
within a noise.

This Ain't Your Kind of Rodeo

Michael Paramo

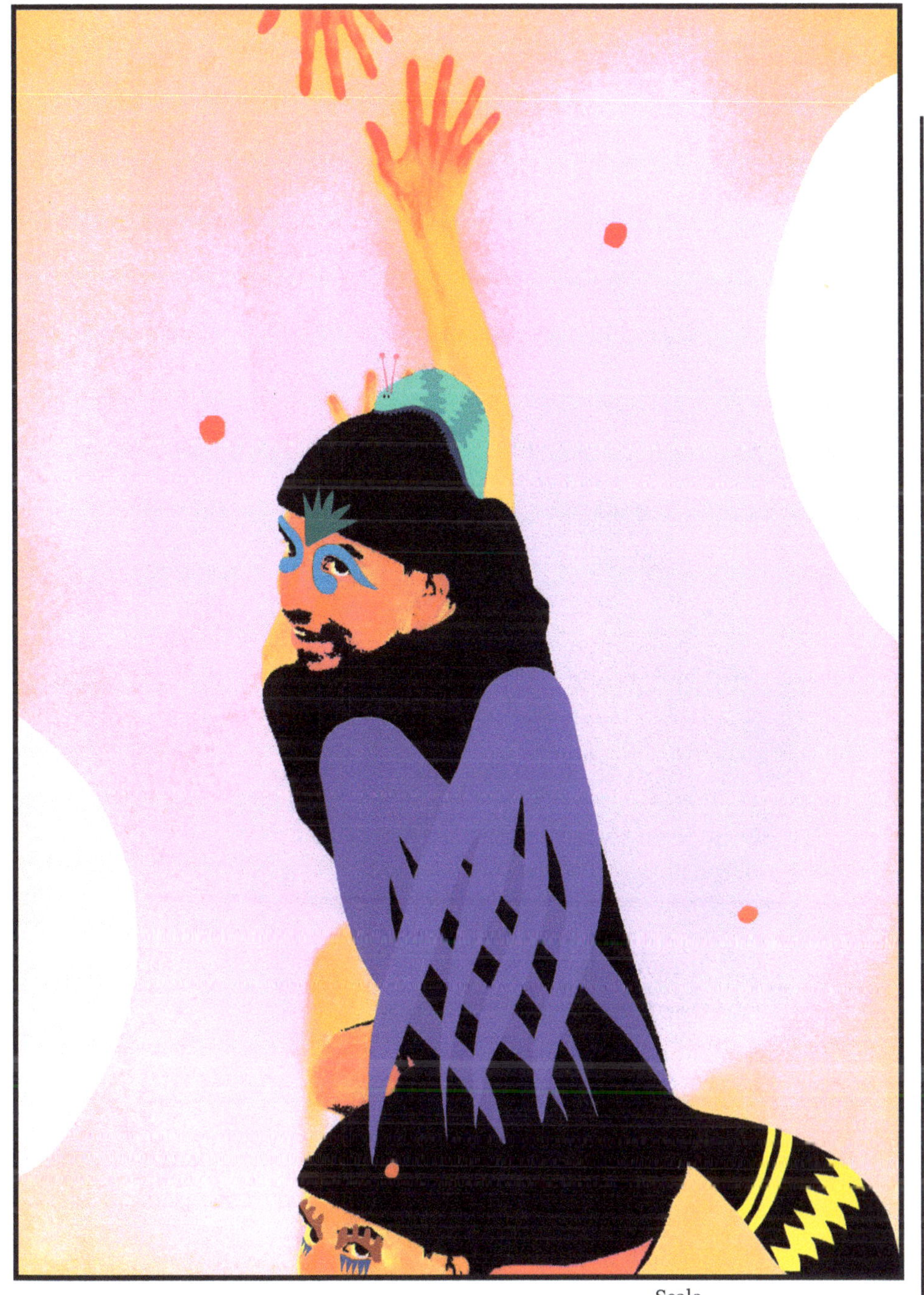

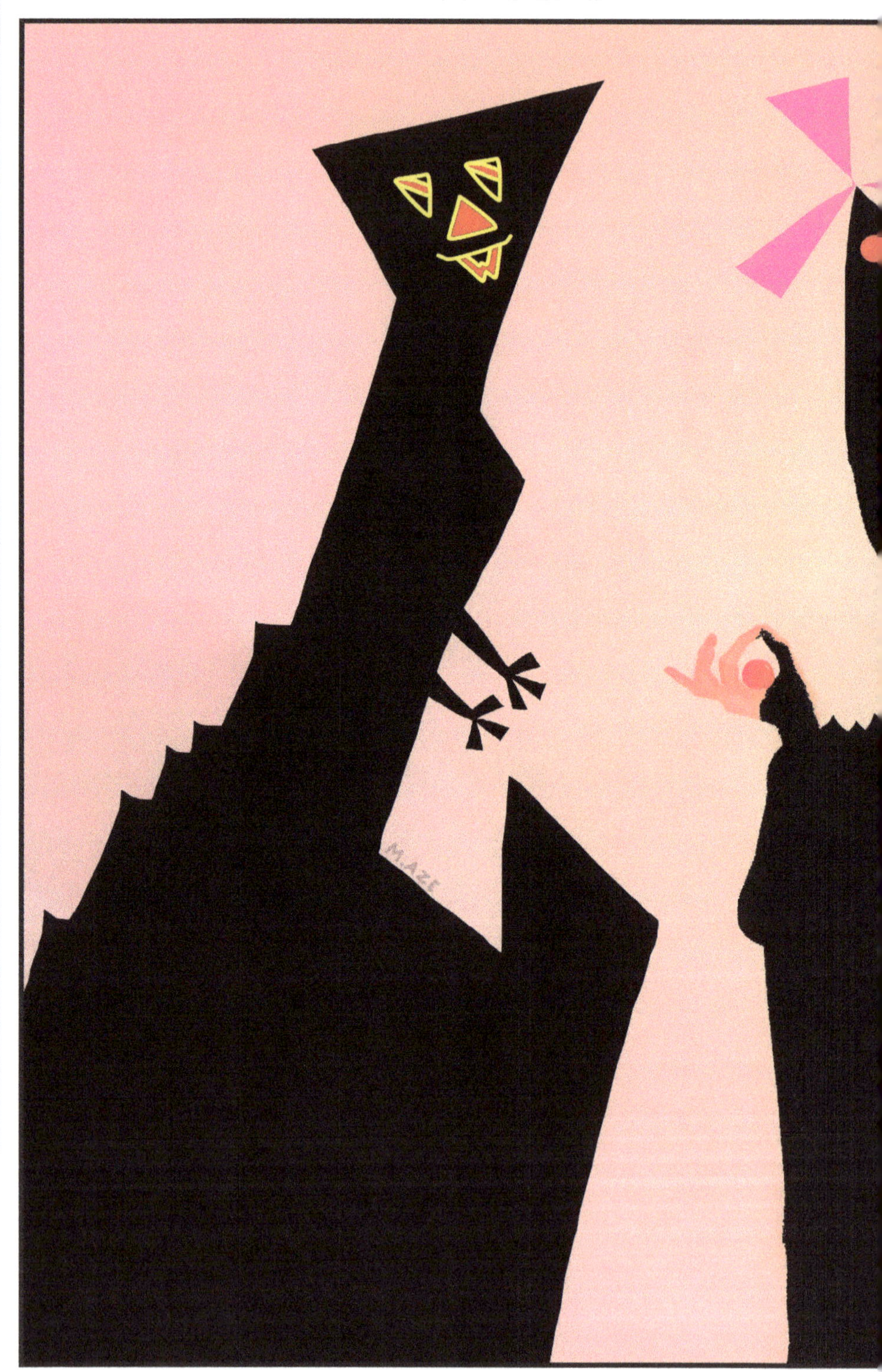

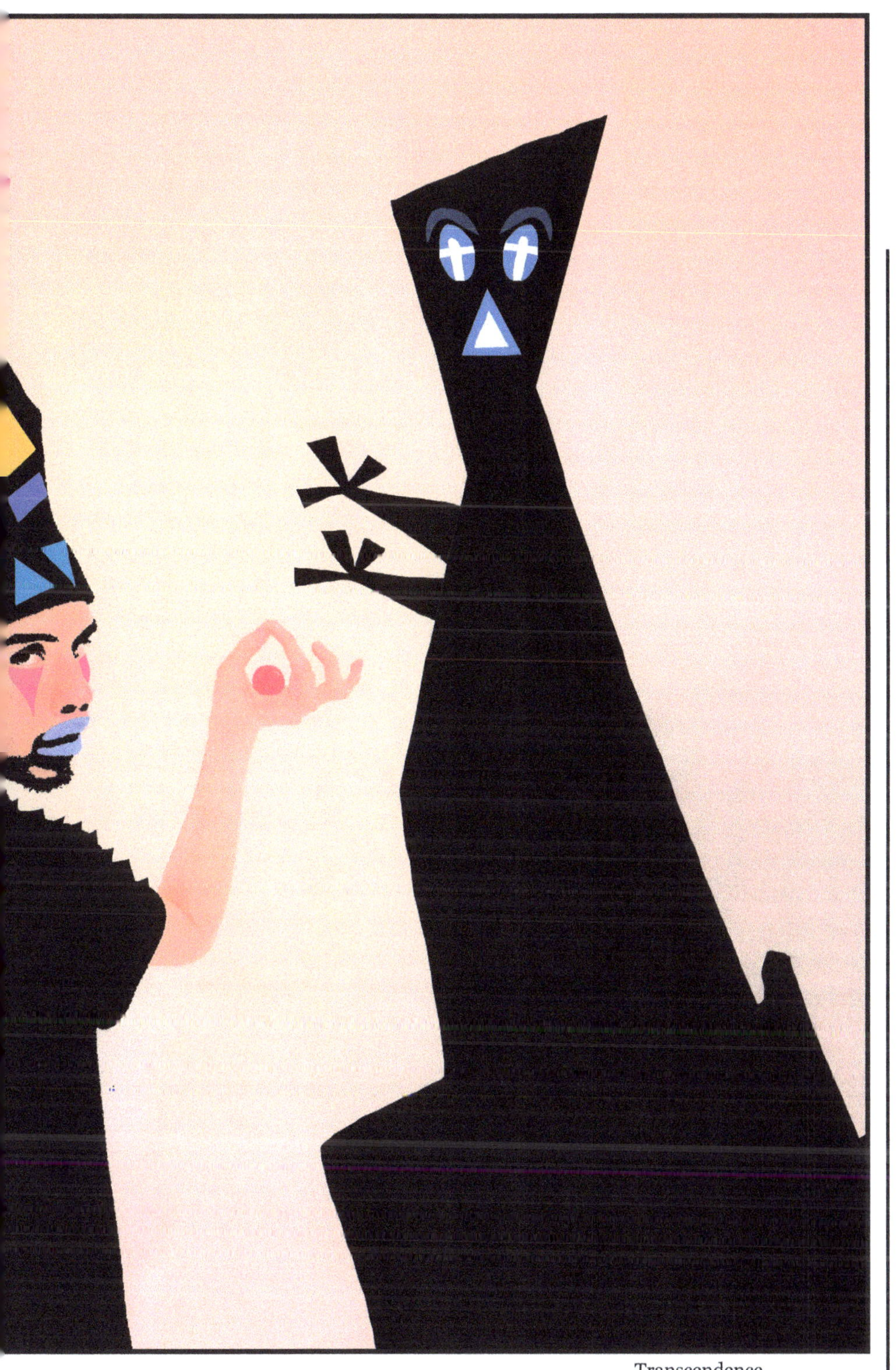

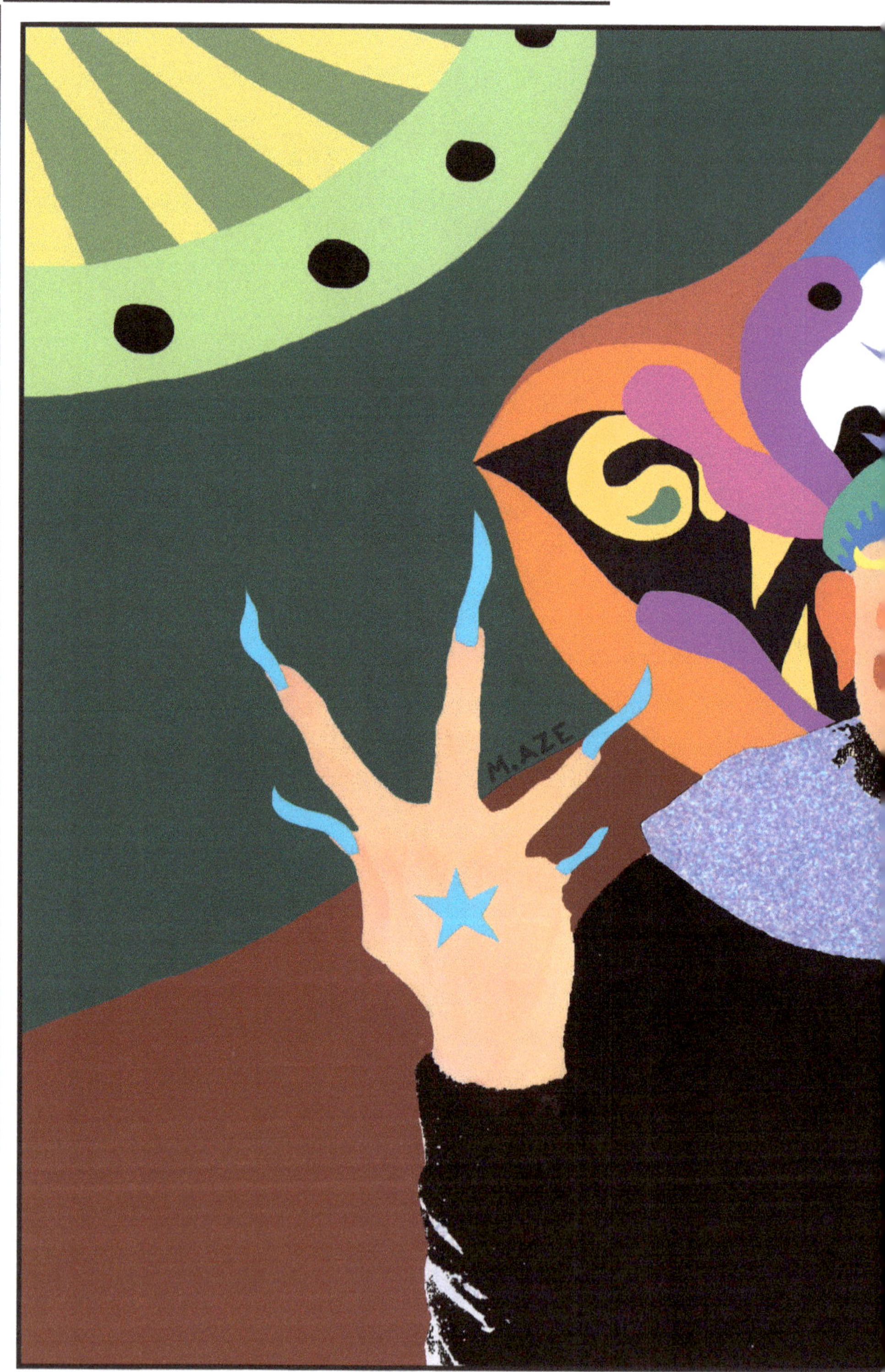

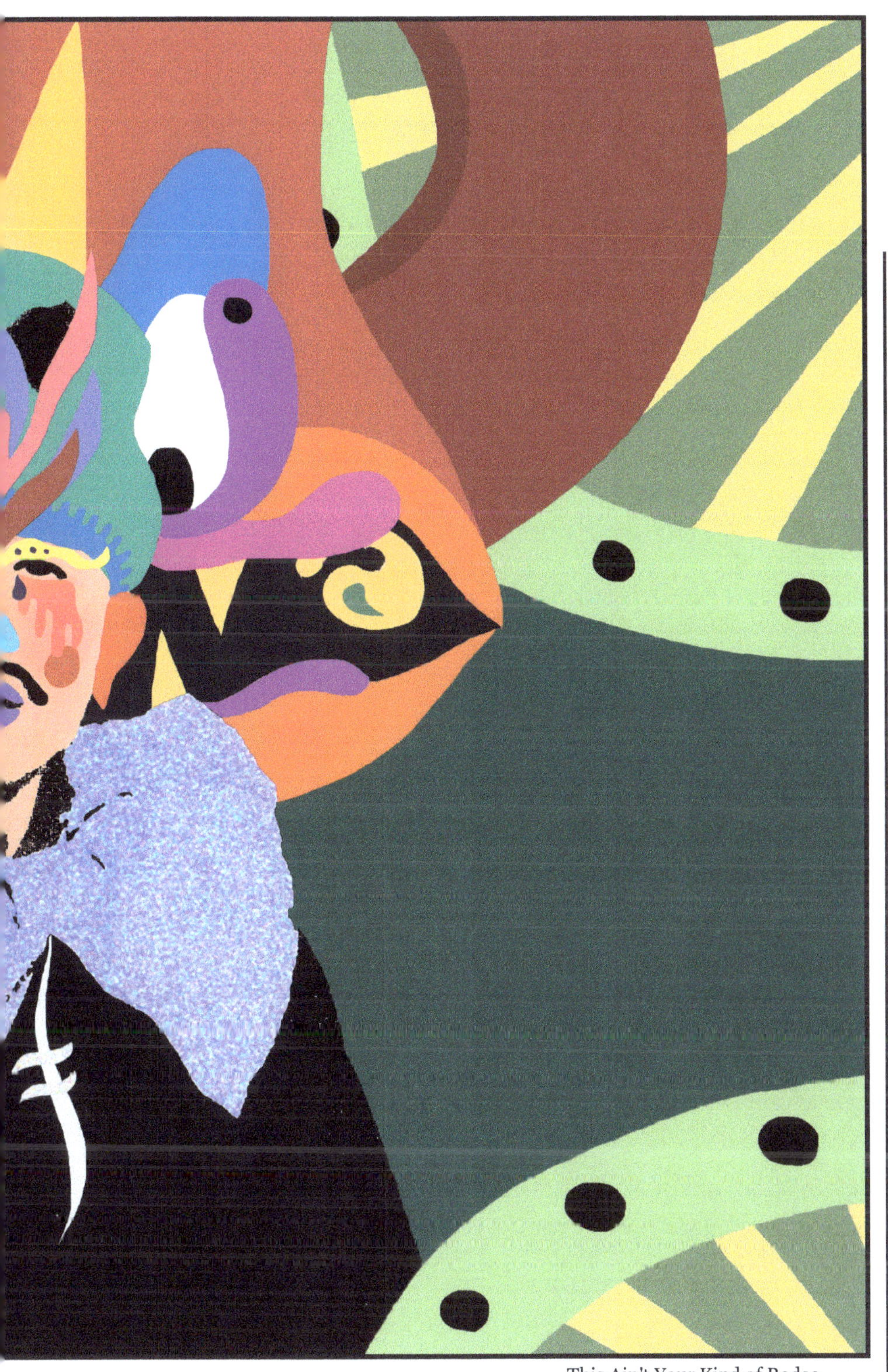

Reasons not to panic if your pharmacy is out of hydroxychloroquine

Vanessa Able

With the nation's supplies of hydroxychloroquine dwindling, we get creative with other failsafe, research-based cures to COVID-19:

Bleach

Bleach is the first battalion in the war against pandemic viruses, the Old Faithful of scientific home remedies. The best thing about bleach is just how versatile it is, both as a preventative measure and a cure. Whether you're feeling the full-blown effects of COVID-related advanced pneumonia, or you're just nursing a scratchy throat, a gallon a day of bleach will set you right as rain and back on the path to Wellsville. Drink, snort or shoot it straight into your aorta.

Alcohol

Prefer a lighter, more sociable solution that you can sip throughout the day? Beer, wine and spirits are the obvious choice here, but don't overlook the potential of alcohol-based cleaners, nail polish removers, aftershave, Dayquil, mouth wash and even bug spray. Get creative and make it fun! Shake up a little virus-killer cocktail by pouring the contents of every single bottle of alcohol you've been storing—use a trash can as a receptacle if you need to—then gather the family and chug it frat house-style through a funnel. No need to wipe between turns either—that brew could kill a horse at ten paces.

Chemo

You've used up all the booze and you've chewed through your daily allowance of Lysol from your supermarket. What now? A little out of the box thinking: What's the worst disease in the whole world? Cancer. And we have drugs for that, right? So it follows that what works for the worst disease in the world should also work for not-so-bad diseases like any kind of virus. Cancer drugs like doxorubicin and thioplex are hard to come by if you don't have the Big C, but I've got a buddy with stage 8 pancreatic selling surplus supplies at a decent markdown. PM me and I'll hook you up.

Psilocybin/Ayahuasca

When all else fails, the outright denial of reality is our only remaining re-course. If you are new to mind-altering hallucinogens, I suggest starting by microdosing yourself and your loved ones every hour for the first 48 hours then transitioning into debilitating doses administered by a certified Shaman over Zoom or something. The more you can involve all generations of the members of your household, the more you'll appreciate the effects of all-out tripping balls together and probably and most certainly almost routing pan-demics from your door.

Farewell/Despedida

Felipe Echeverría

A dream, like Icarus, took flight and soared

The rider travels straight paths
    oblivious to the human pain that he drags.

The curtain of time is drawn
            while change floods the streets
and custom entrenches herself
                against the last corners.

            The piano seeks melodies
to weave amidst his white teeth

While aspiration on her unicycle
        balances upon the taunted rope
                of the horizon at dusk.

Within this rider's heart, an unending tune:

I am kite chaser,
    zenith who thrusts himself unto the storm,
                and the steppe pilgrim

I am rocking caravel
awaiting the vastness of the sea
            and the silence of the stars

I am sailor who cannot find land,
        alone
            in his vessel upon the sea

My body is ethereal foam
            and my soul, homeless wind.

Selene sighs
    at tears which imbue my eyes,
            tears for a distant dream
        dock which reached will not be.

Why do I sadly crave land
        when the sea is so beautiful?
            Will my thirsty heart
                    ever be quenched?

My lips, wet and pale,
        Tremulously refuse to speak
        But my eyes reply
            with their nostalgic shine

        Flux before dreams,
            my nest
        but a solemn vestige.

Un sueño se escapó y voló muy alto

El jinete atraviesa los espejos
De cacerías transparentes
Con dolores humanos

Ya se descorre el telón de los años
El momento inunda las calles
Y la costumbre se atrinchera
Ante las últimas esquinas

El piano busca melodías
Que se tejan entre sus dientes blancos
Han perdido su brújula
Nuestros relojes mancos

El deseo en su monociclo
Recorre la cuerda tensada
Del horizonte atardecido

En el acantilado
El péndulo recita su canción:

Yo soy el perseguidor de cometas
El risco que se lanza a la tormenta
Y el peregrino de la estepa
Soy la oscilante carabela
Que aguarda ante la vastedad del
mar
Y el silencio de la estrella.

Yo soy el marinero que no encuen-
tra tierra,
solo, en su bajel sobre la mar.
Mi cuerpo es etérea espuma
y mi alma, viento sin hogar.
En mis ojos se han visto lágrimas,
que a Selene hacen suspirar.
Lloro por un sueño lejano,
puerto que no puedo alcanzar.

¿Por qué ansío triste la tierra,
si tan bonita está la mar?
¿Es que mi corazón sediento,
jamás podrá saciado estar?

Mis labios, húmedos y pálidos,
trémulos se niegan a hablar;
más mi mirada responde
con su nostálgico brillar.

Antes del sueño está la muerte
Nido
Vestigio   solemne

Envisage

Denise M Oehl

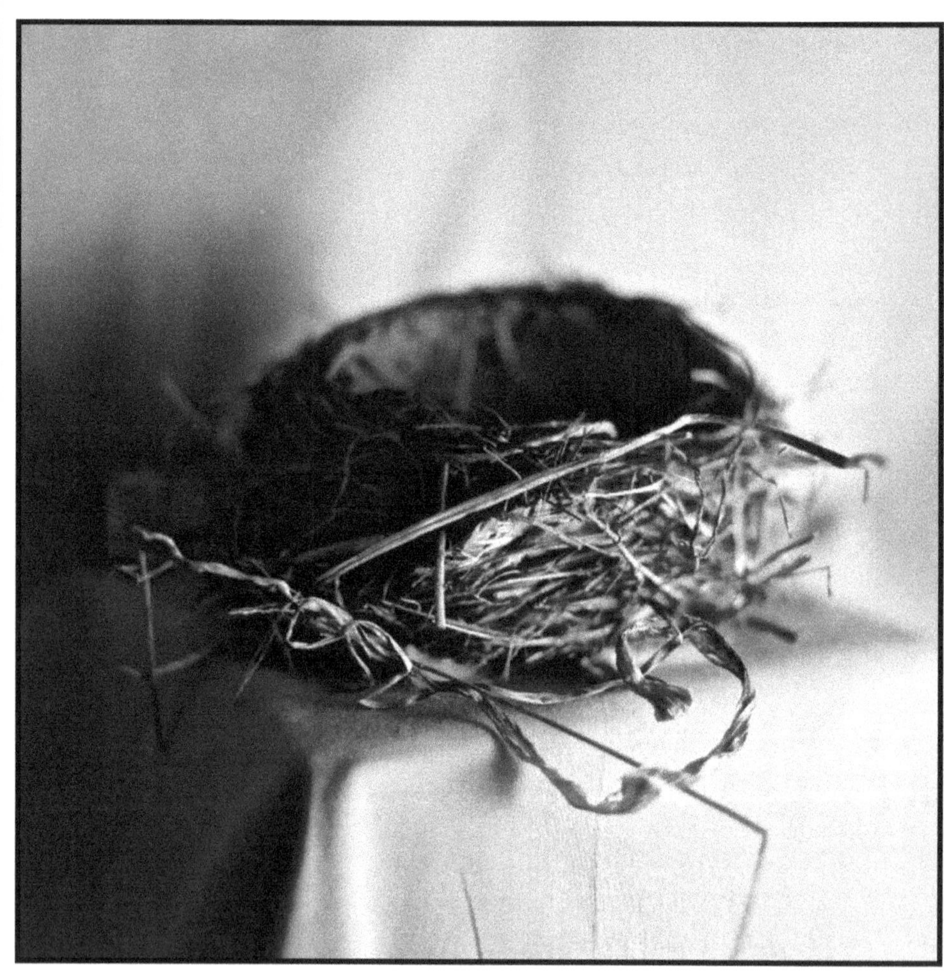

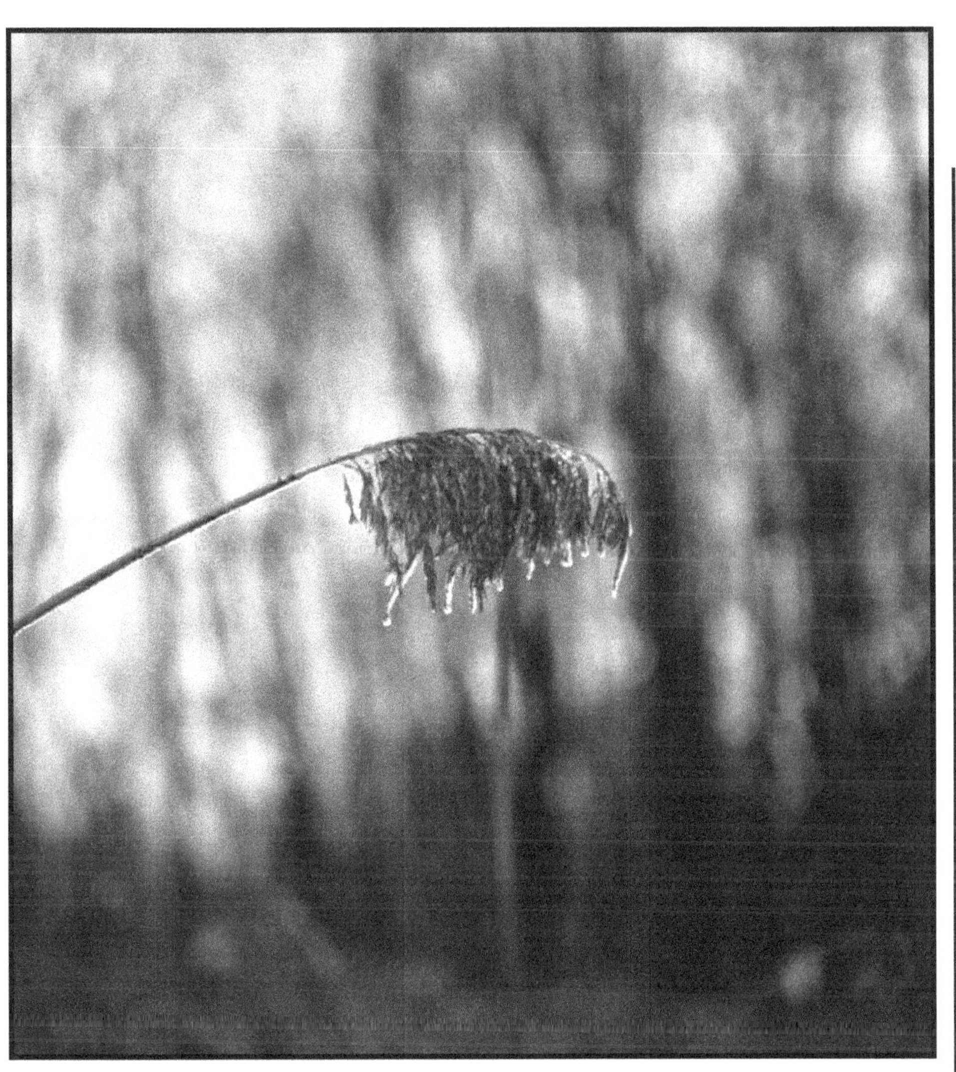

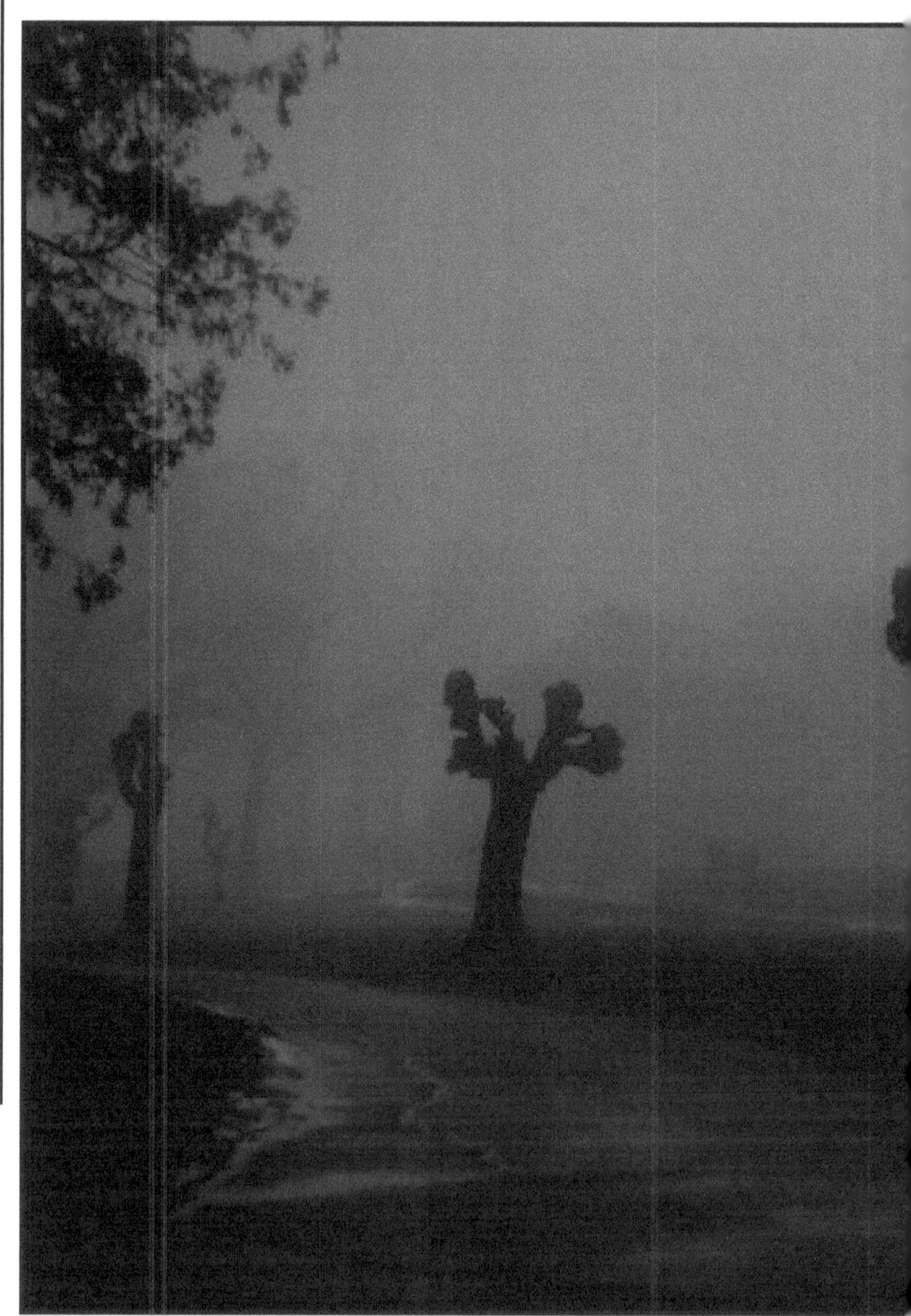

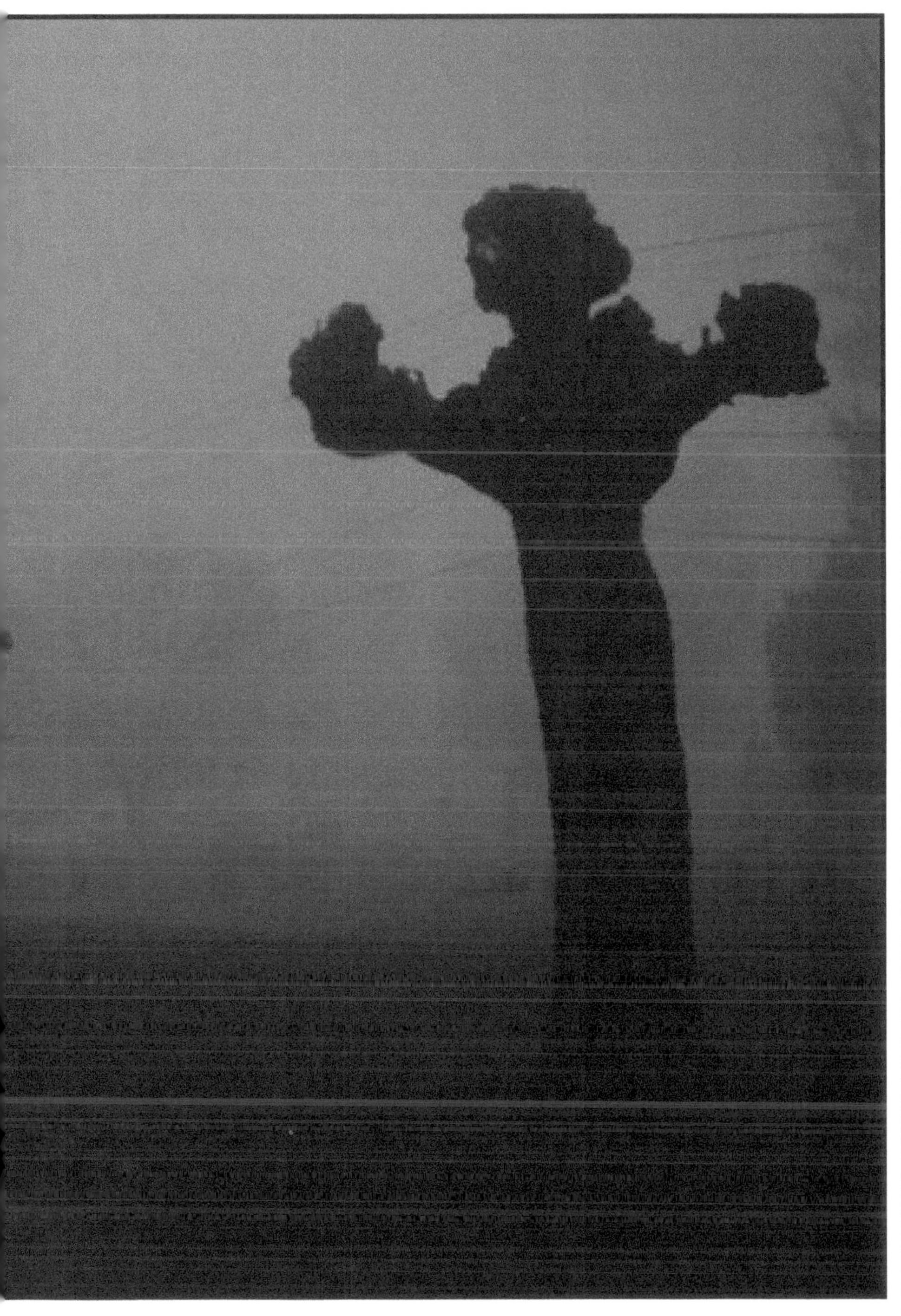

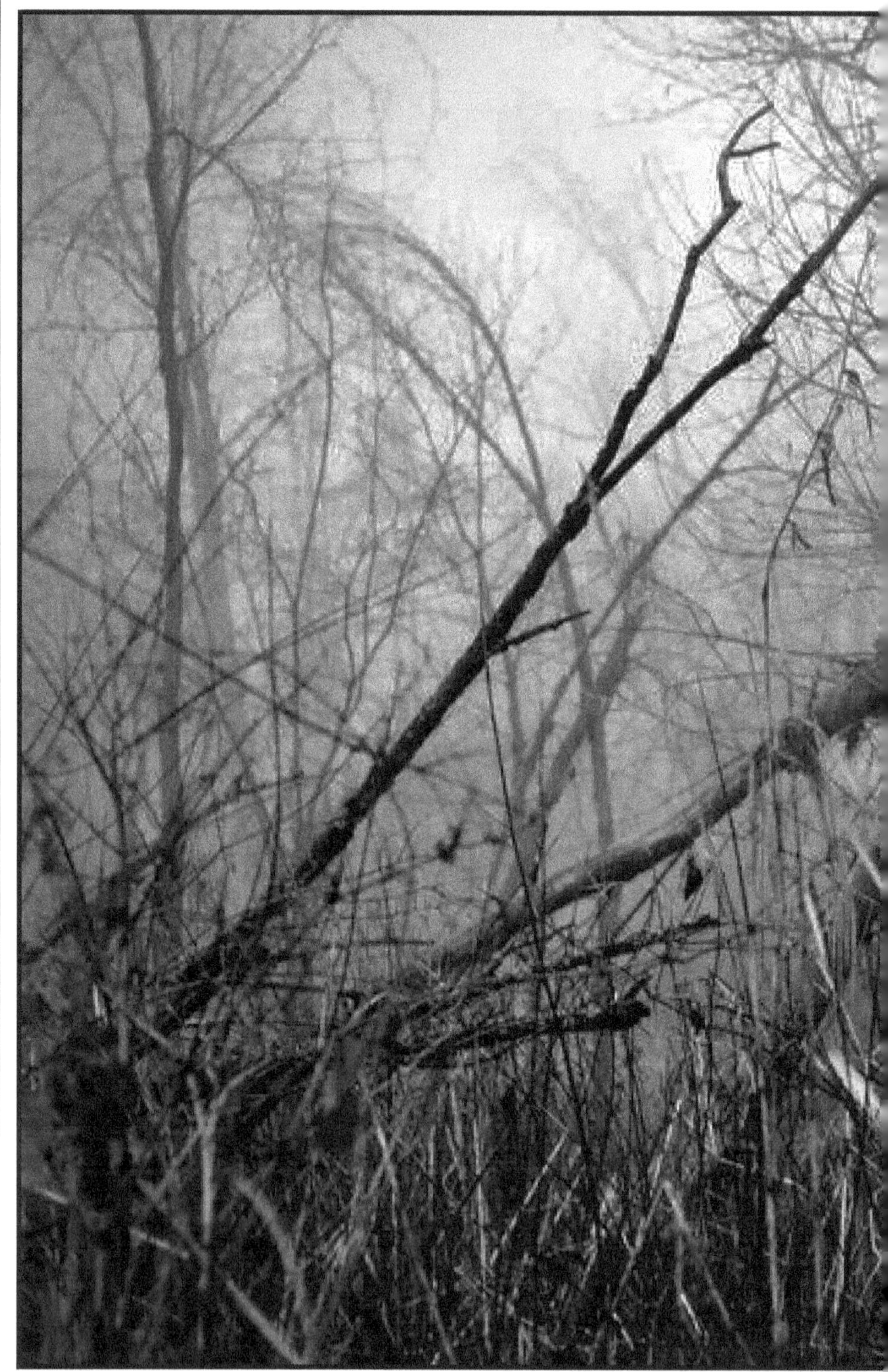

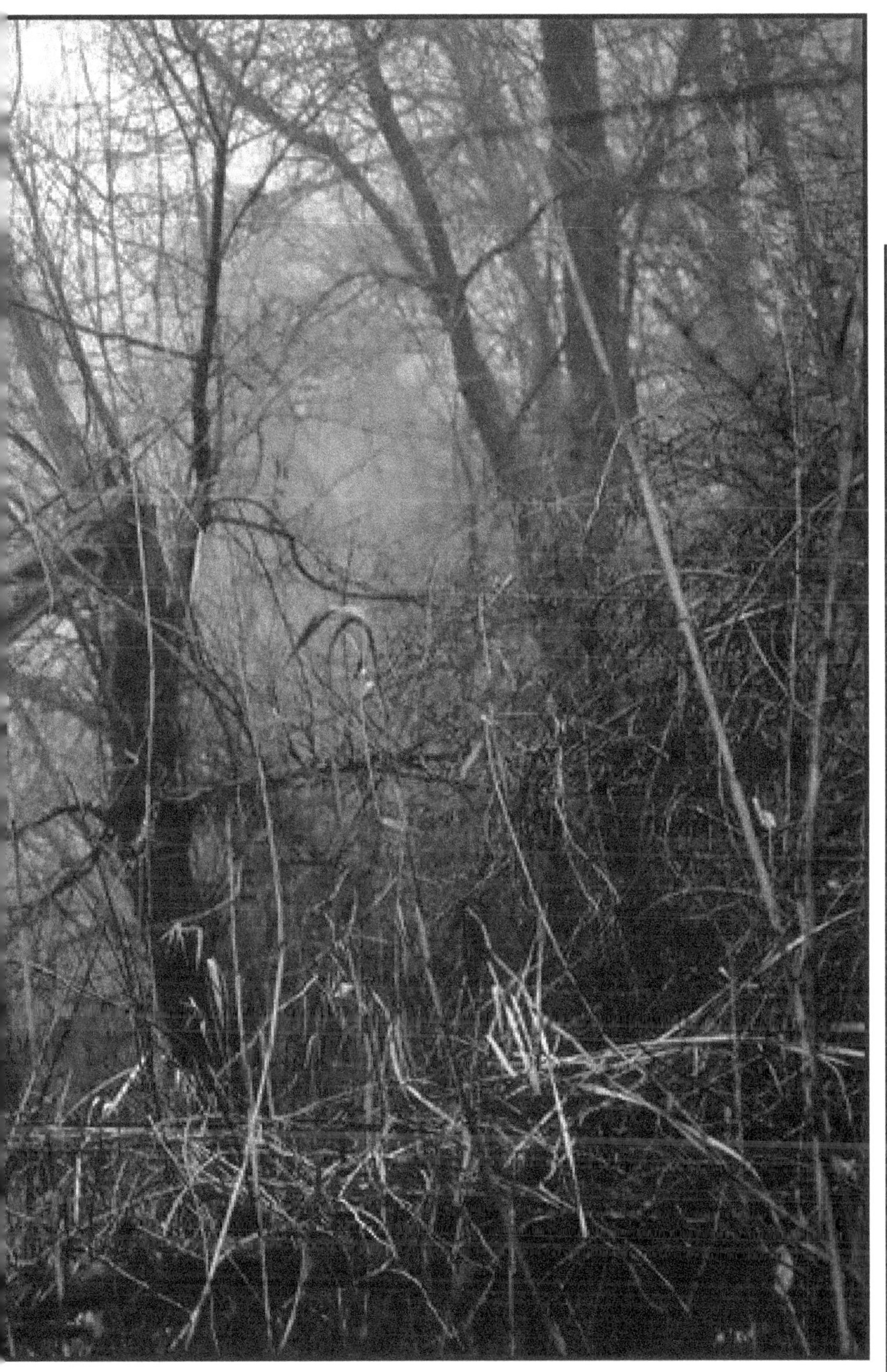

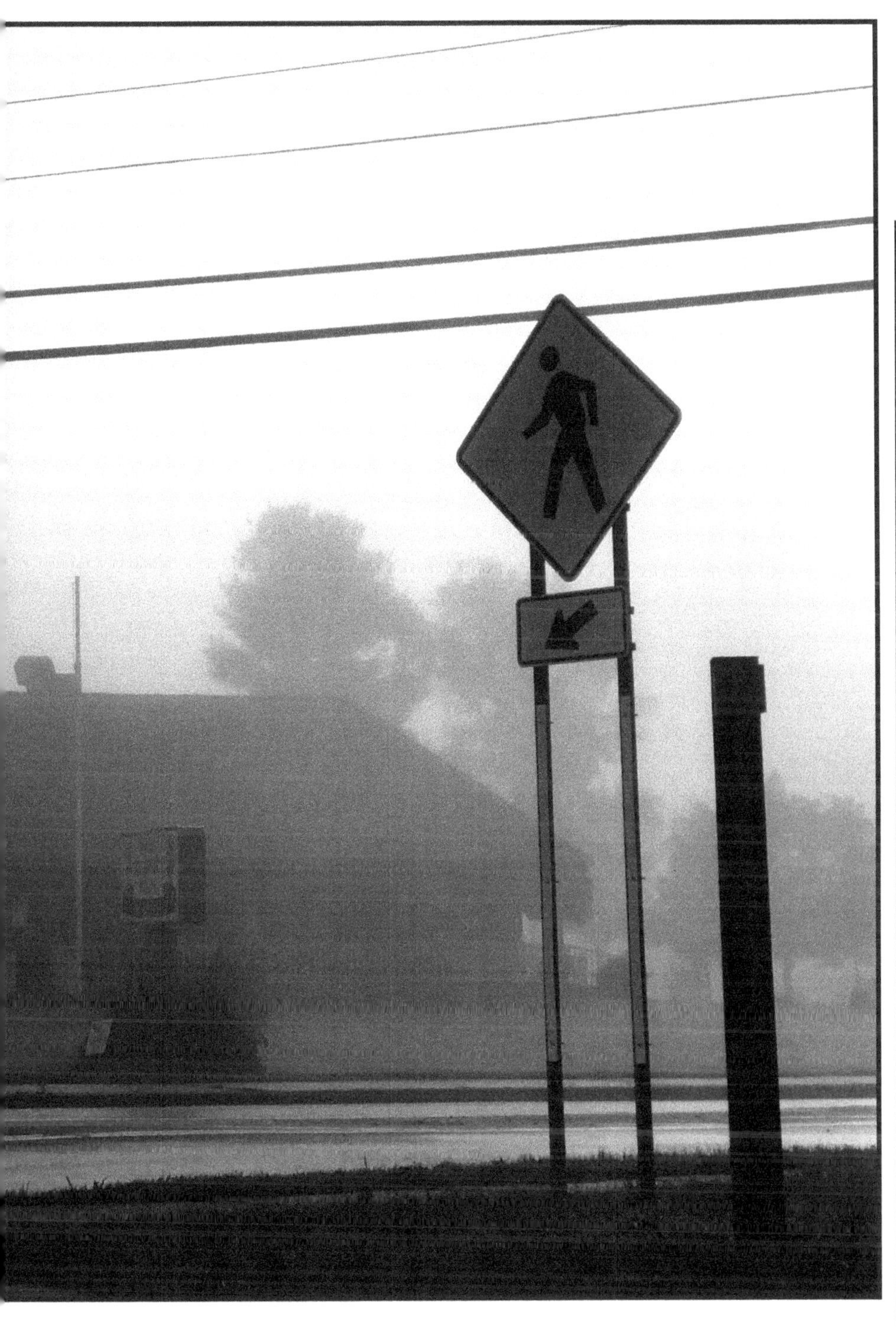

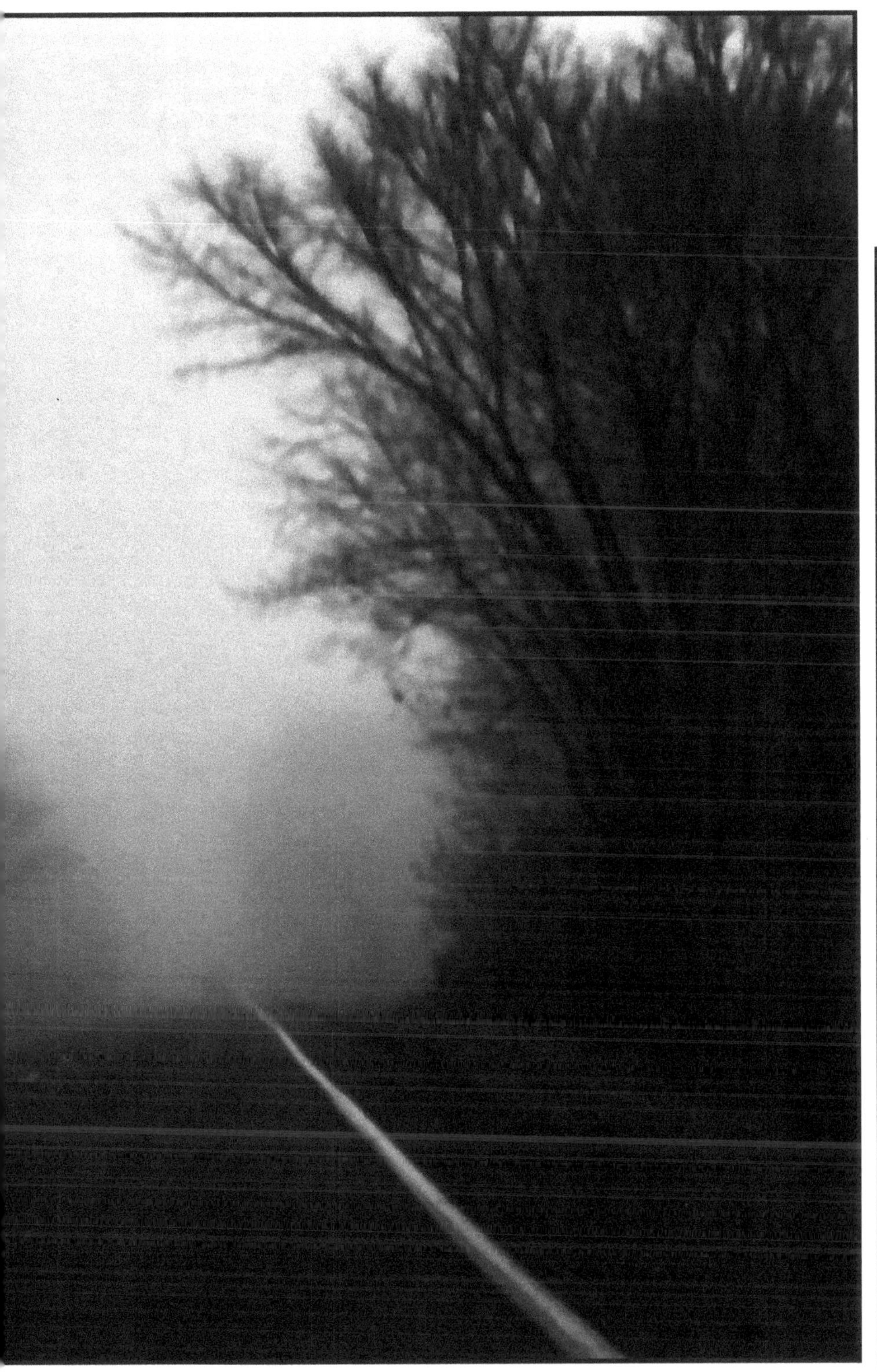

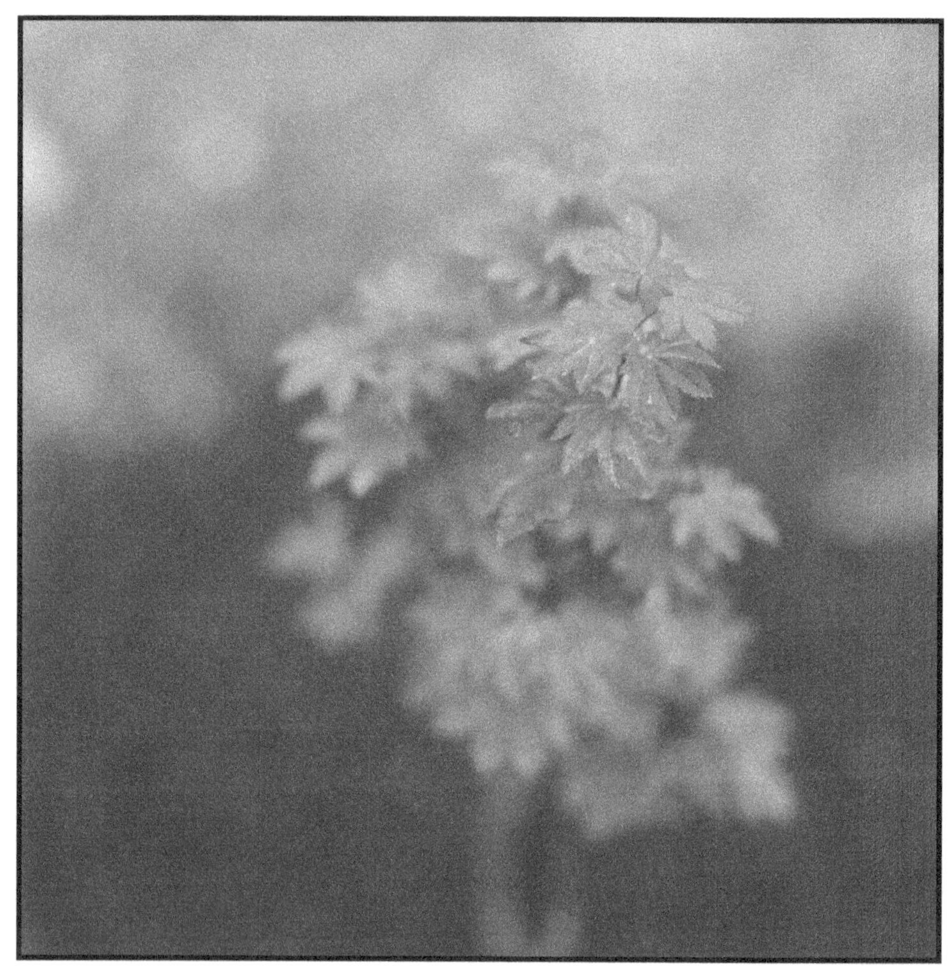

50

Steelworks

Michael Hower

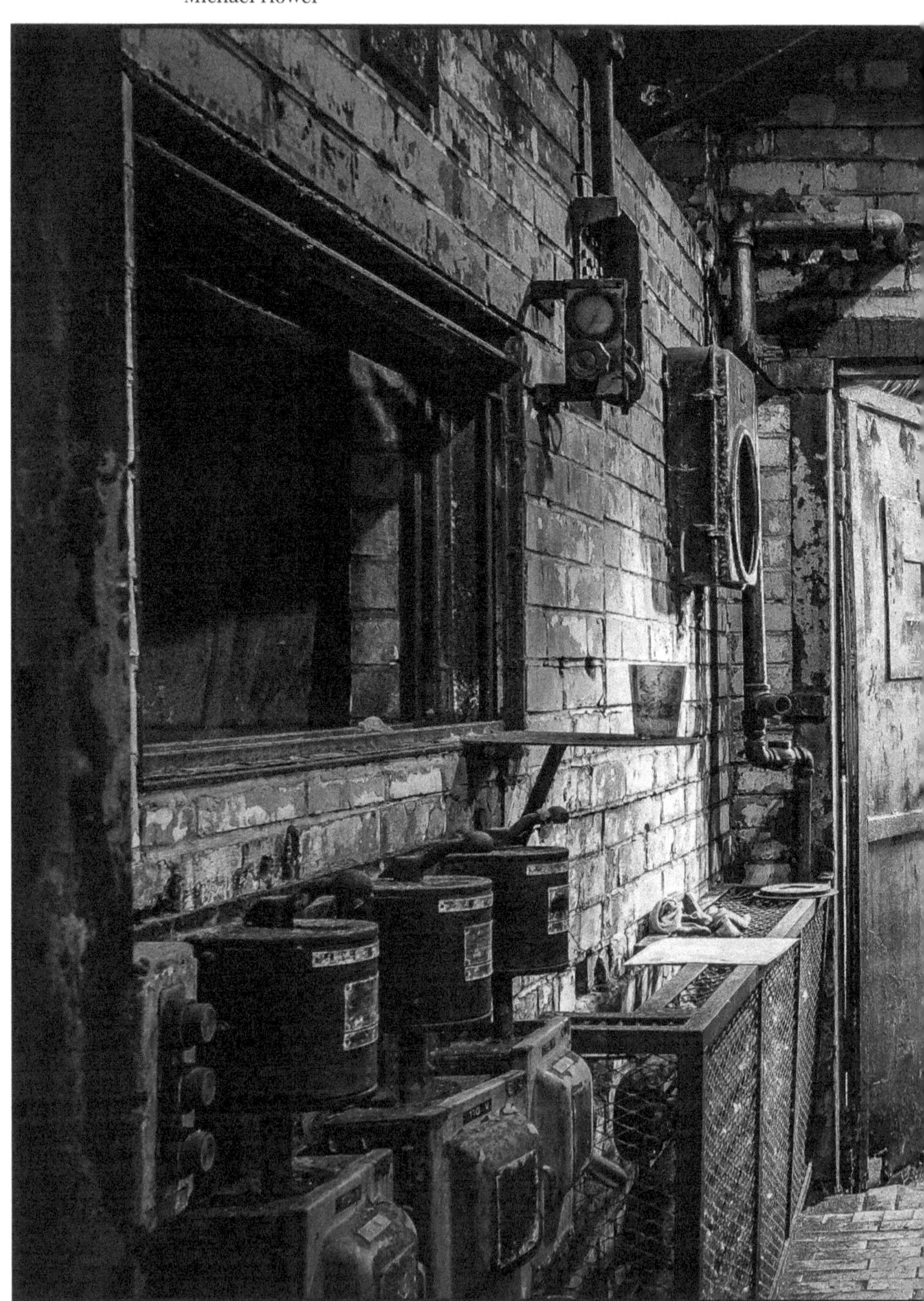

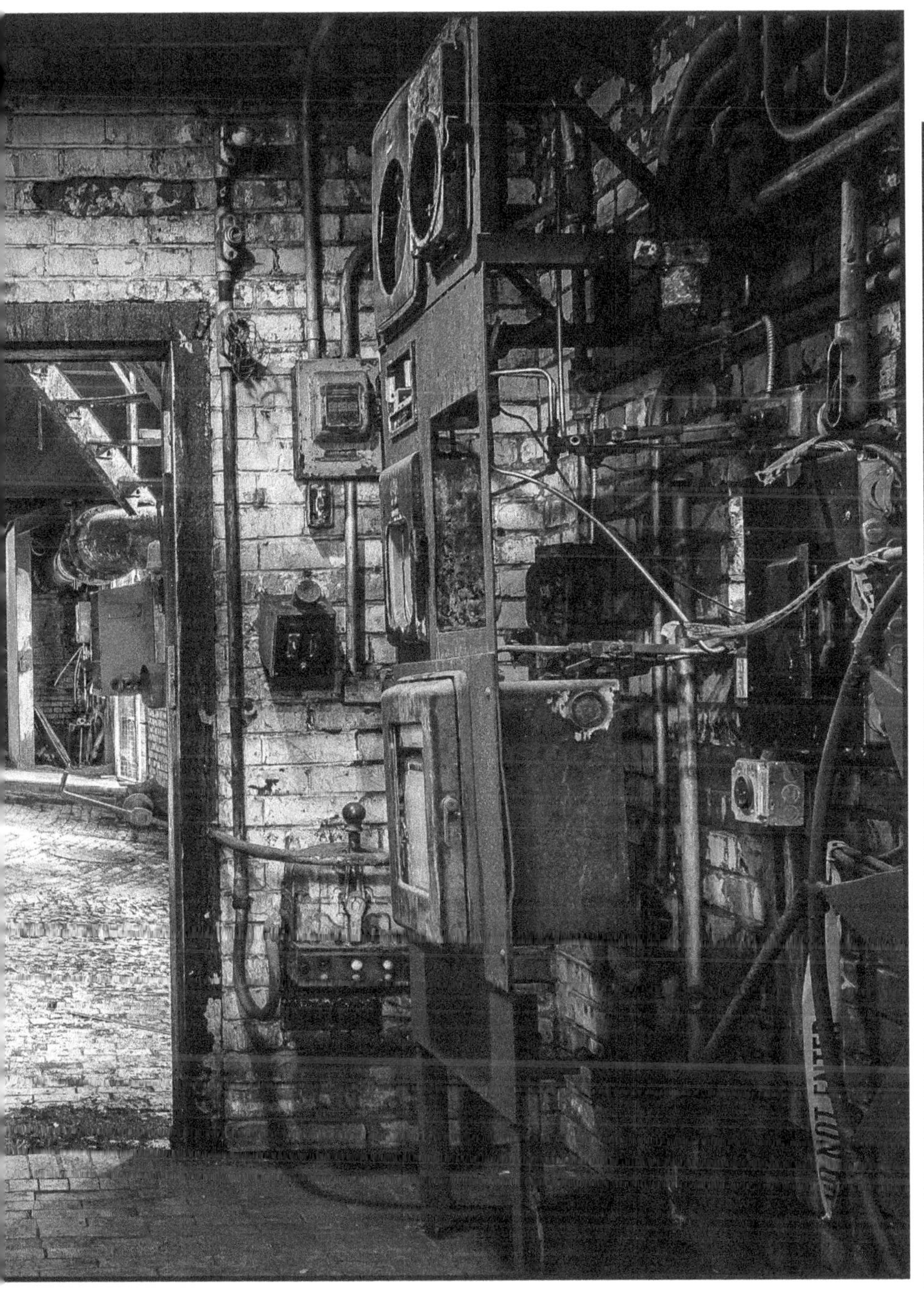

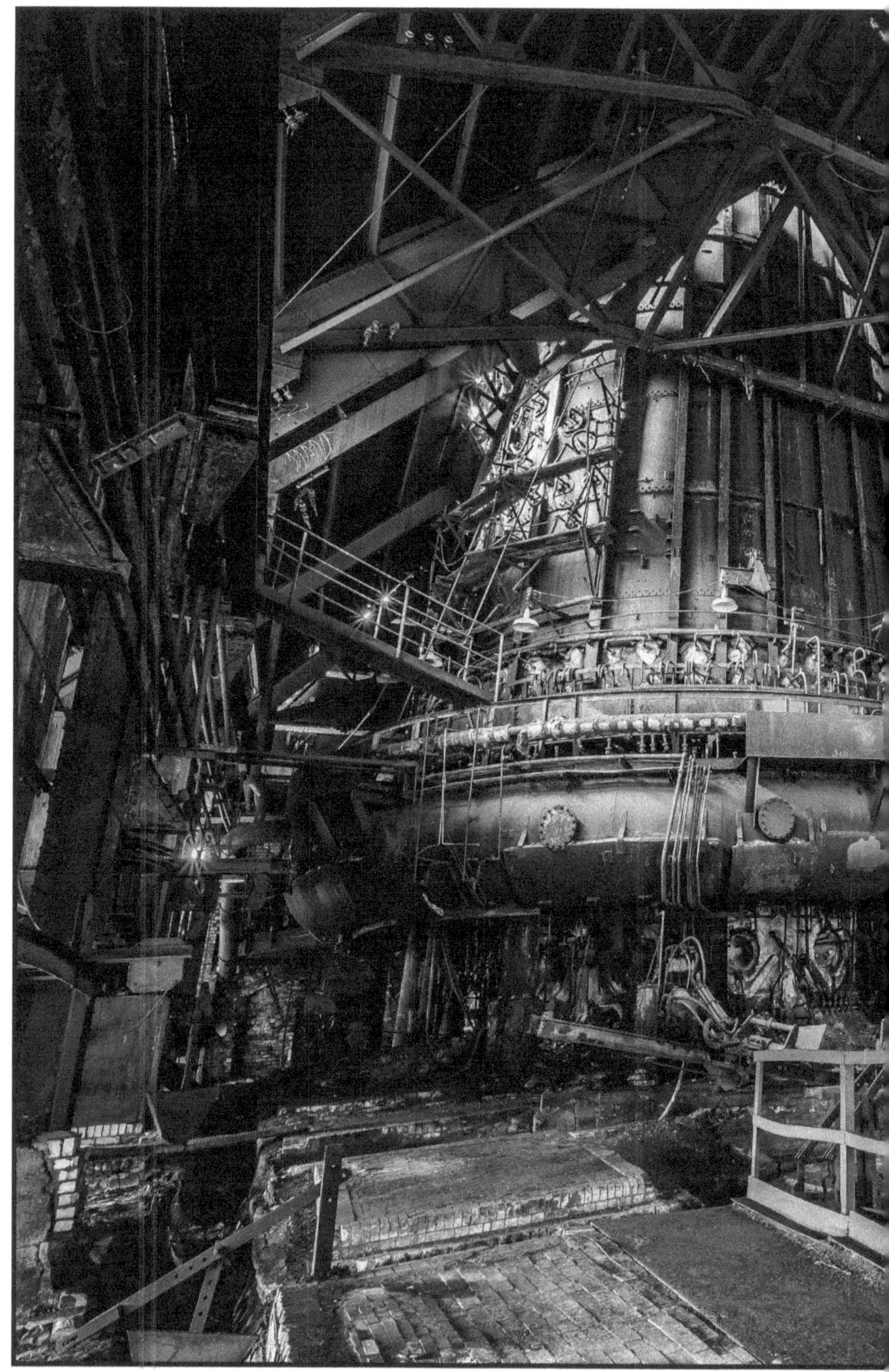

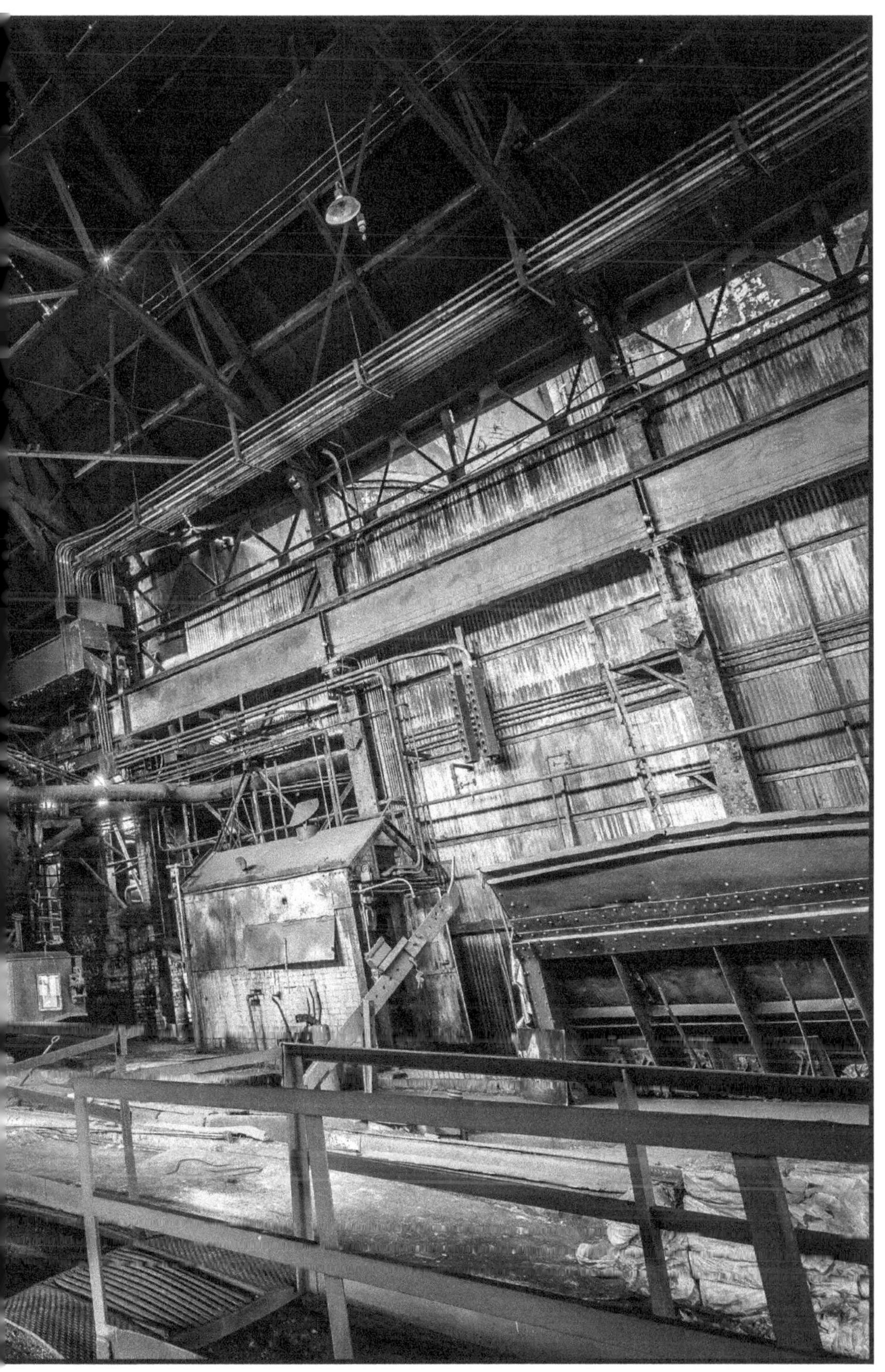

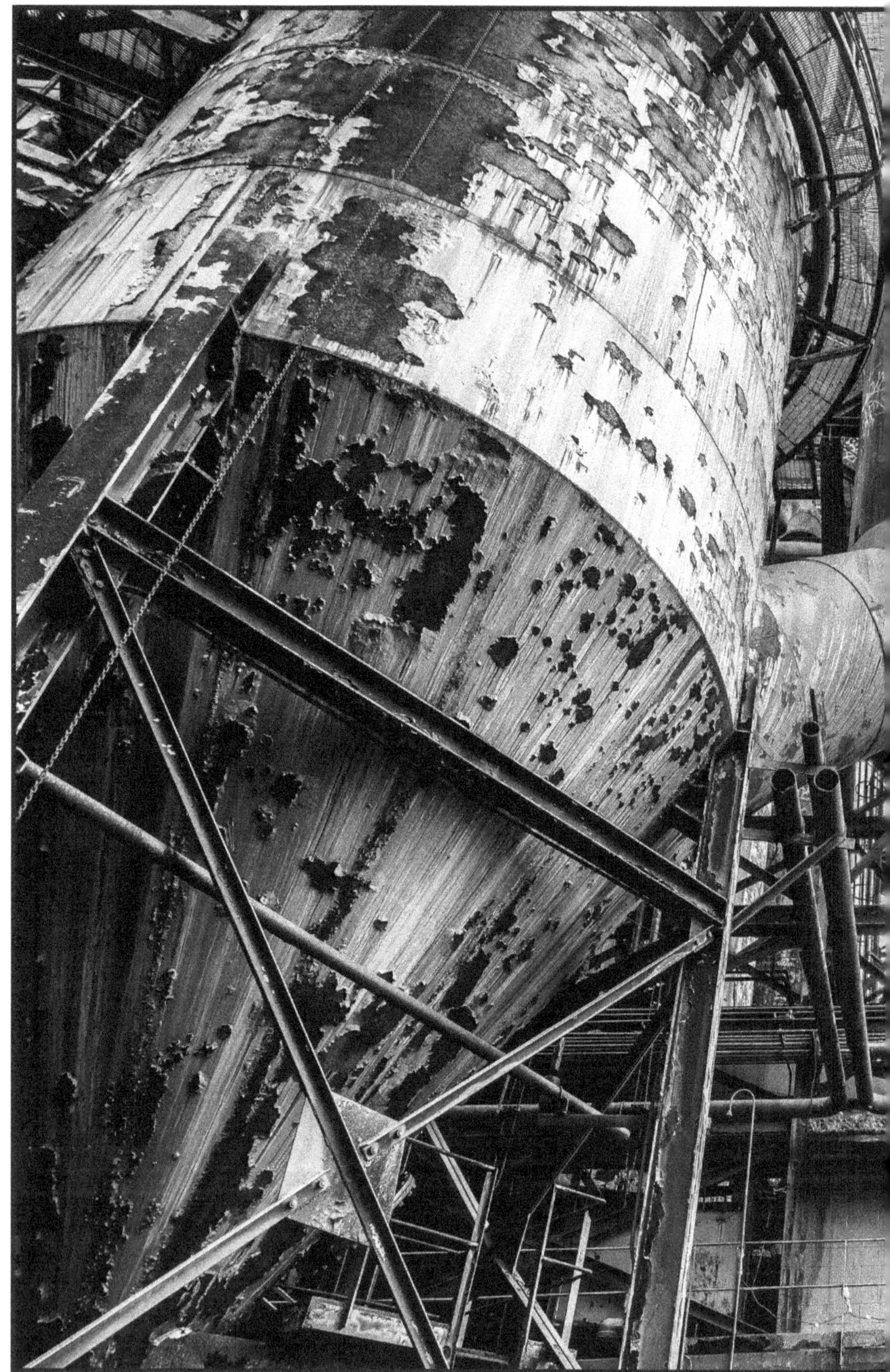

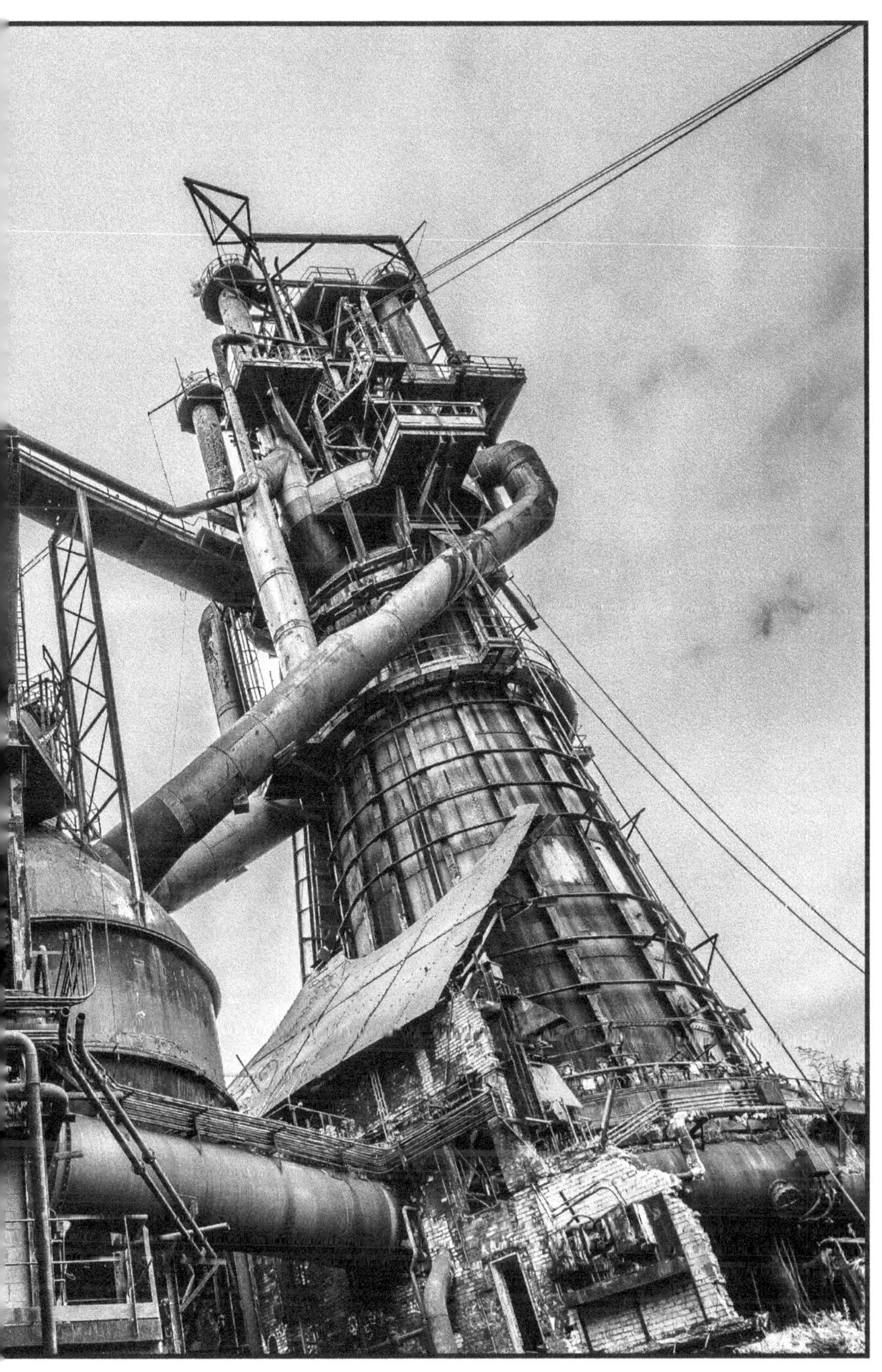

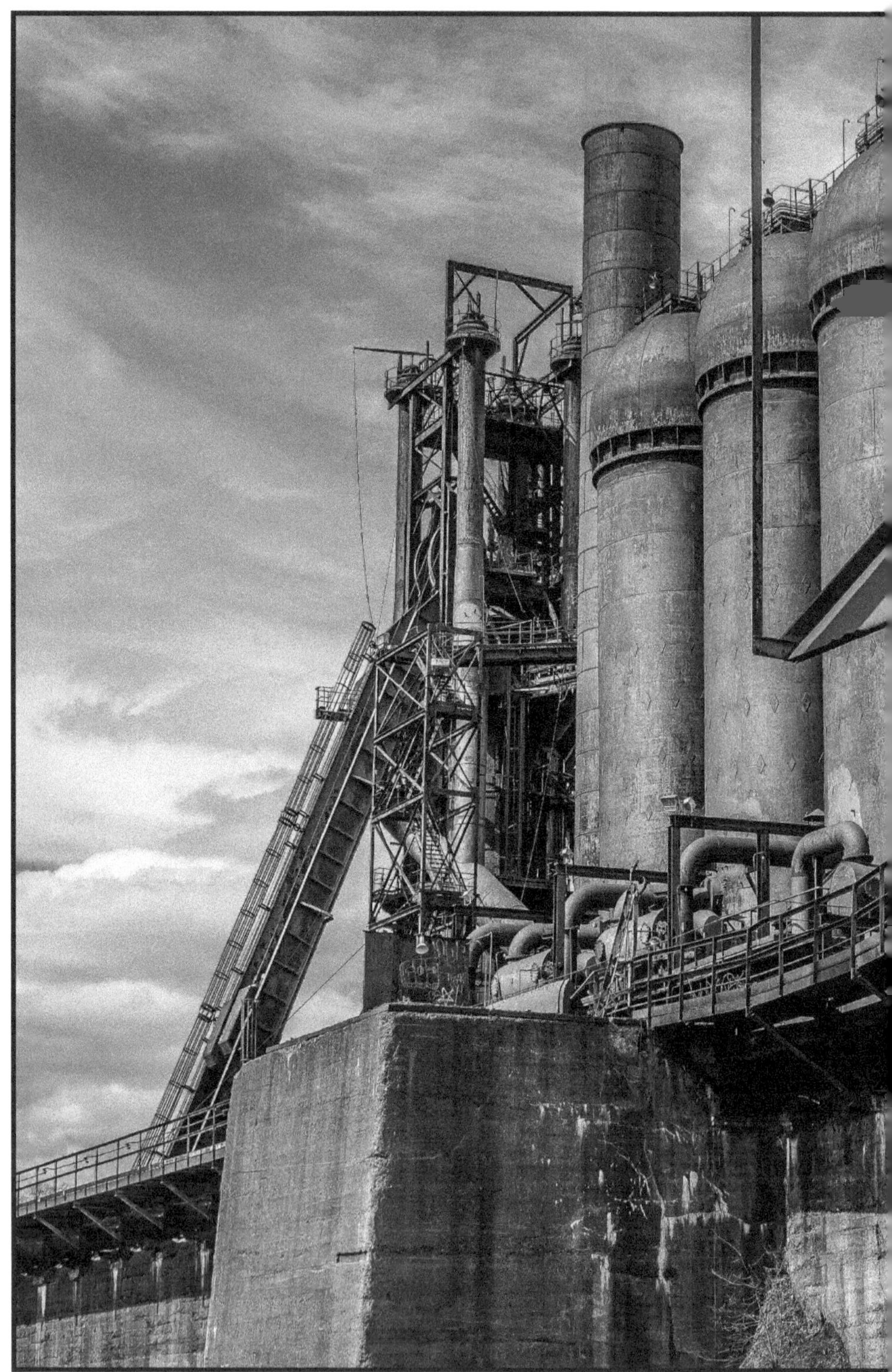

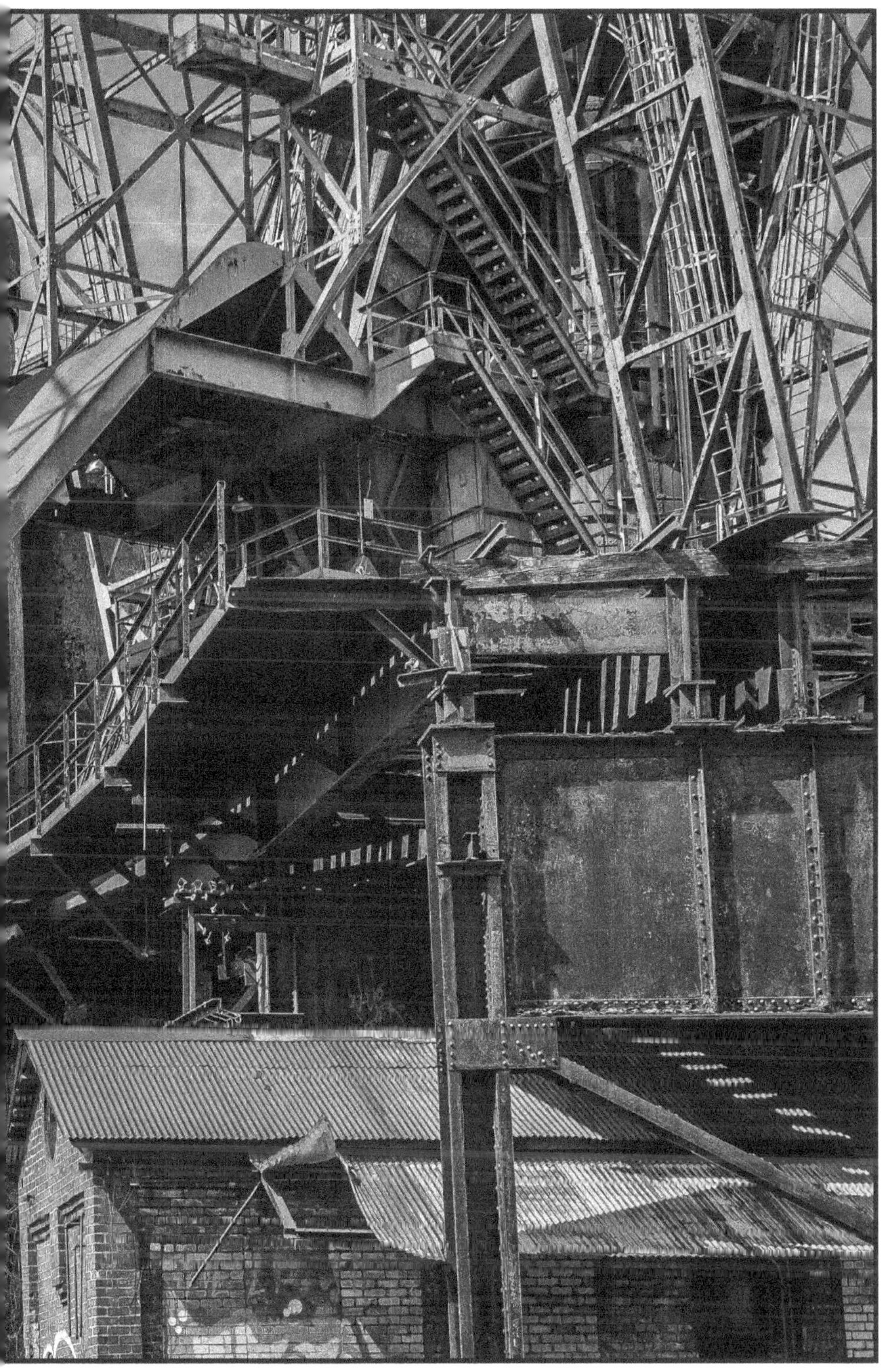

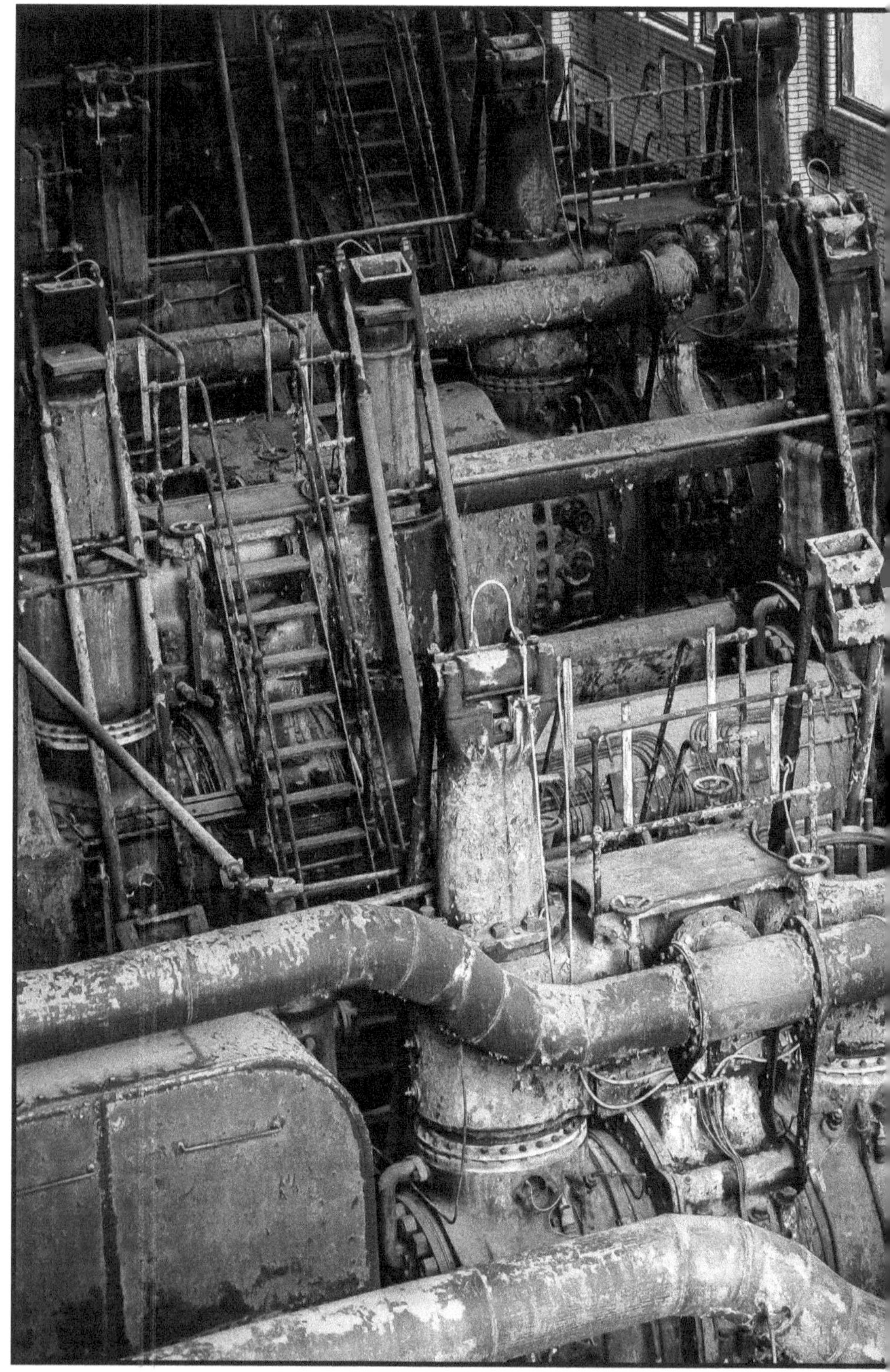

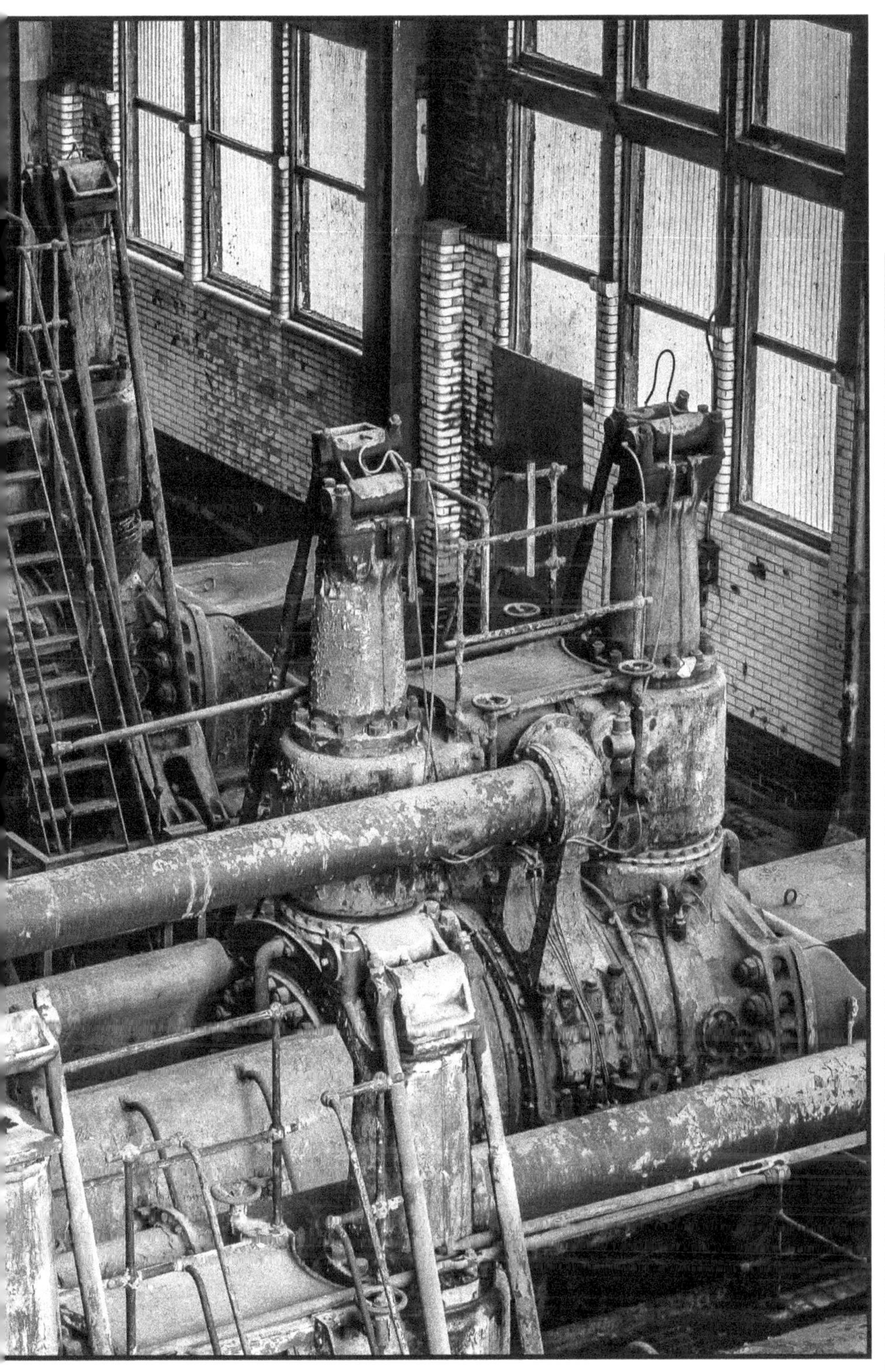

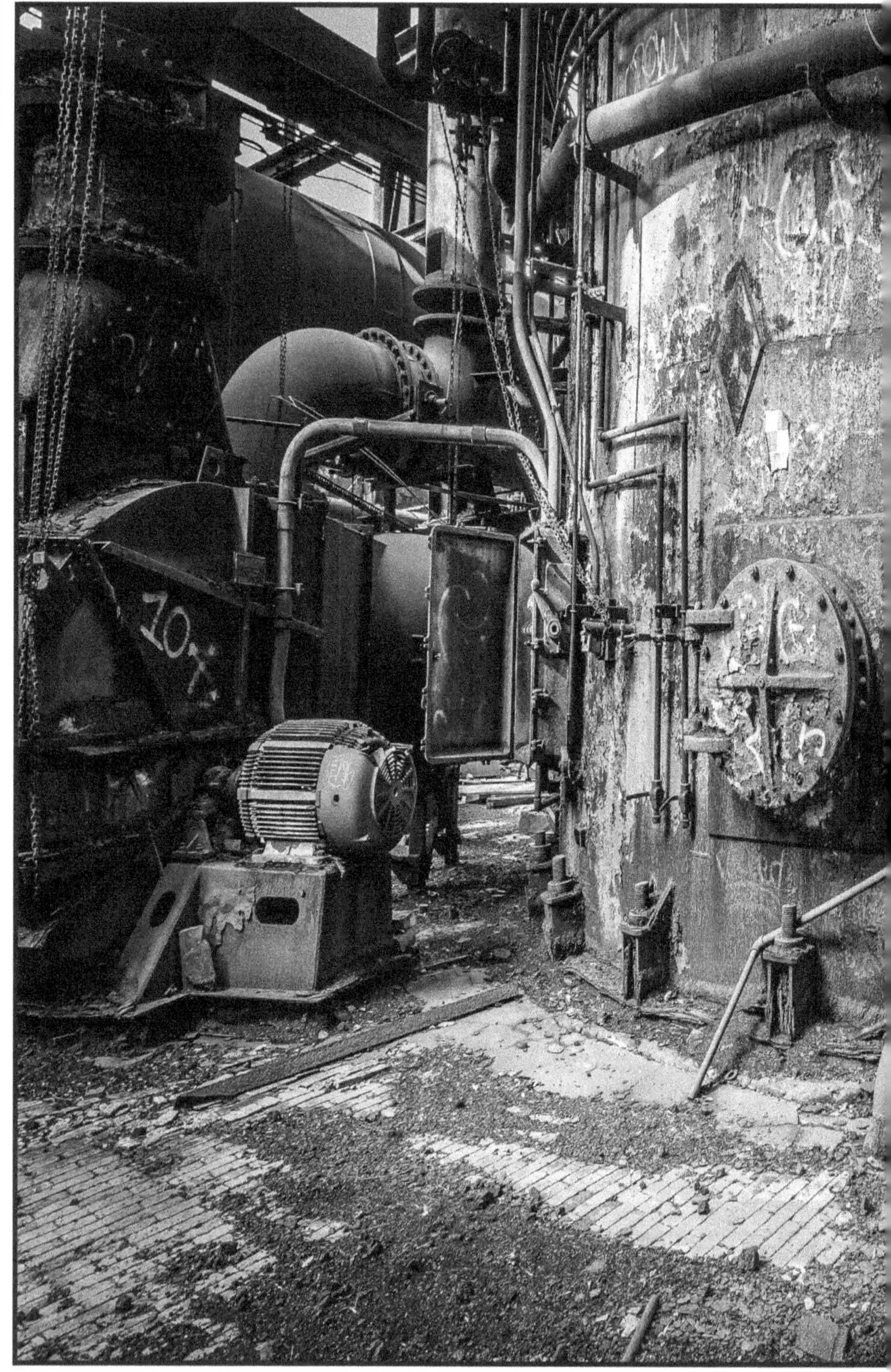

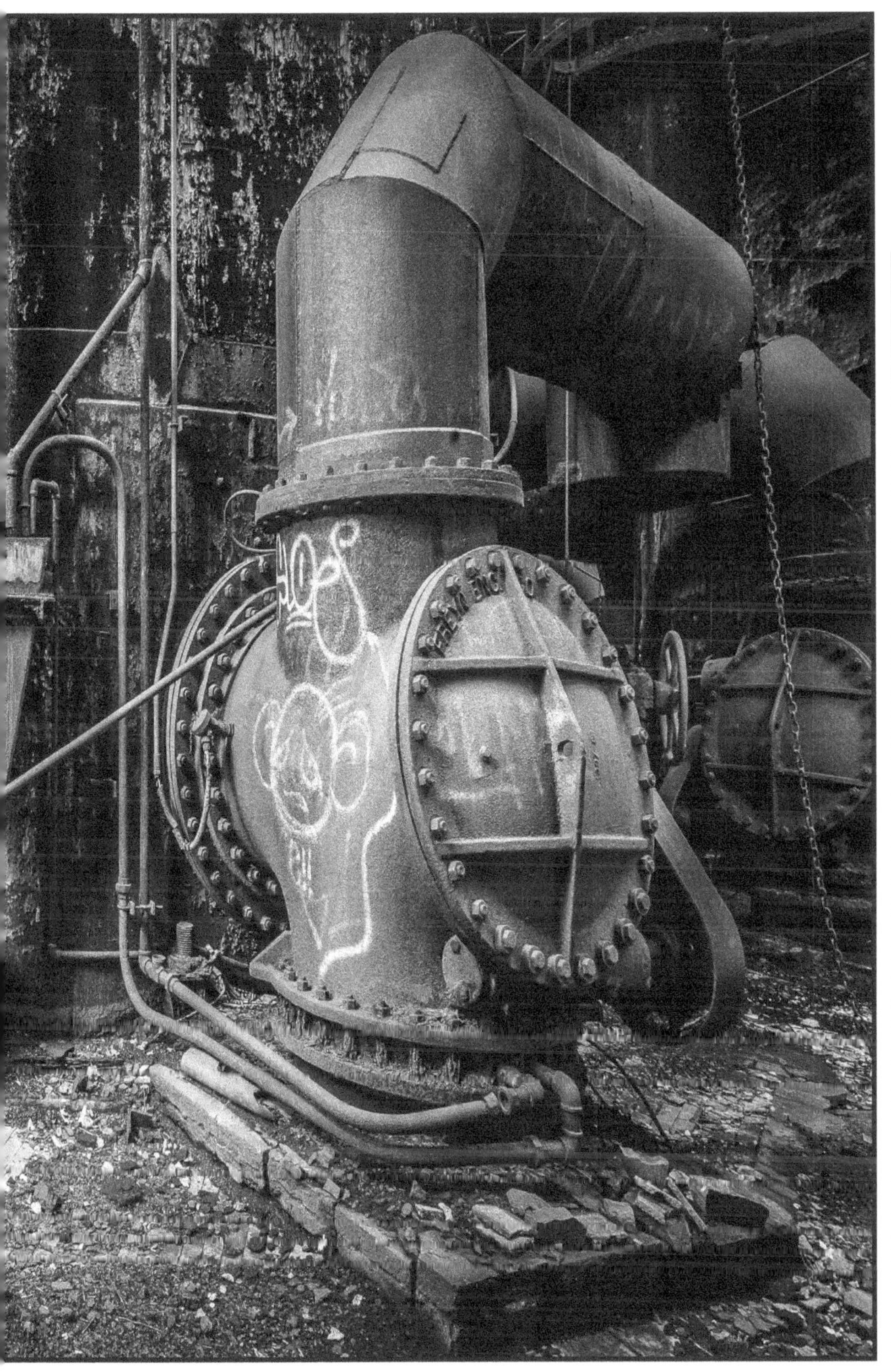

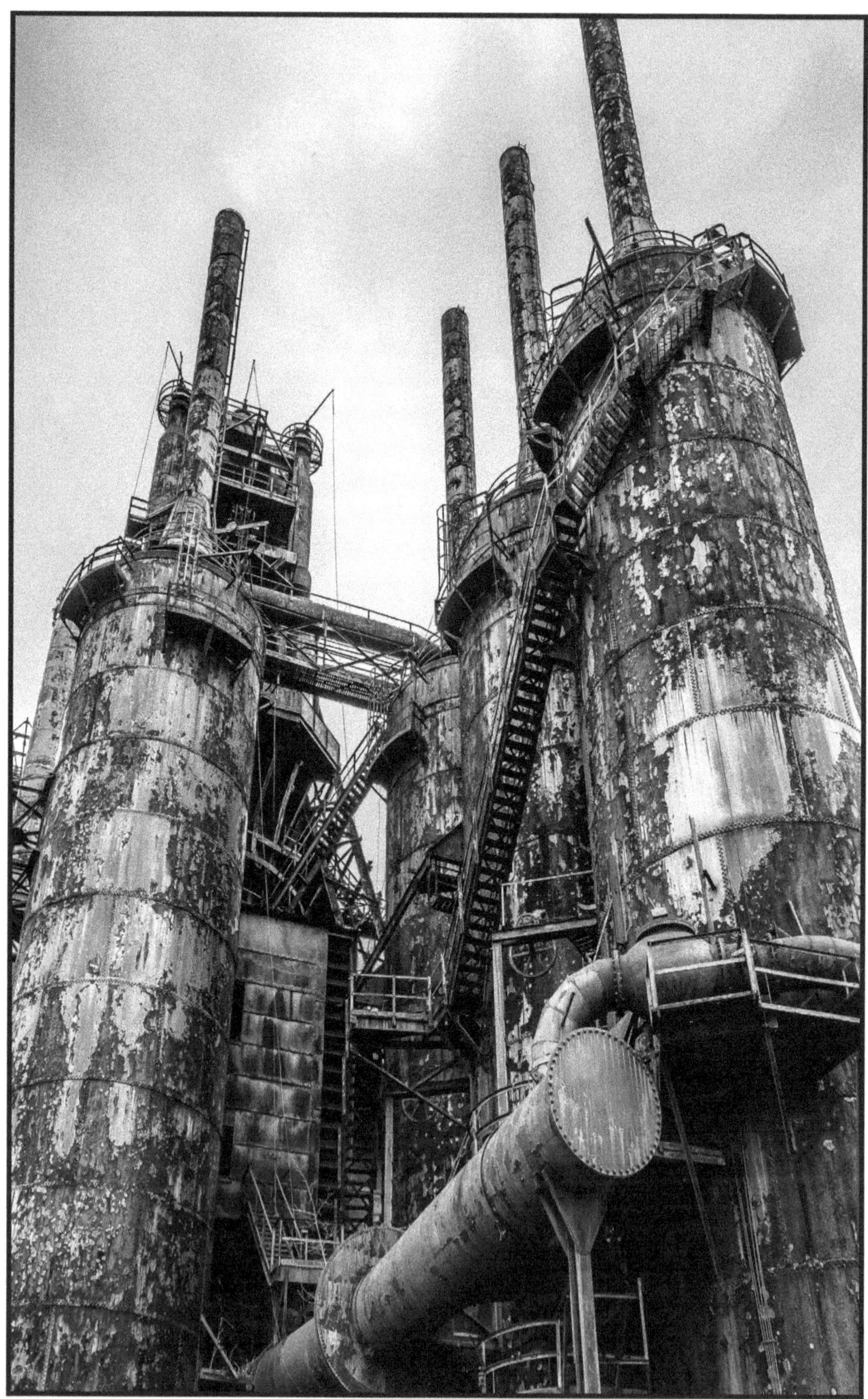

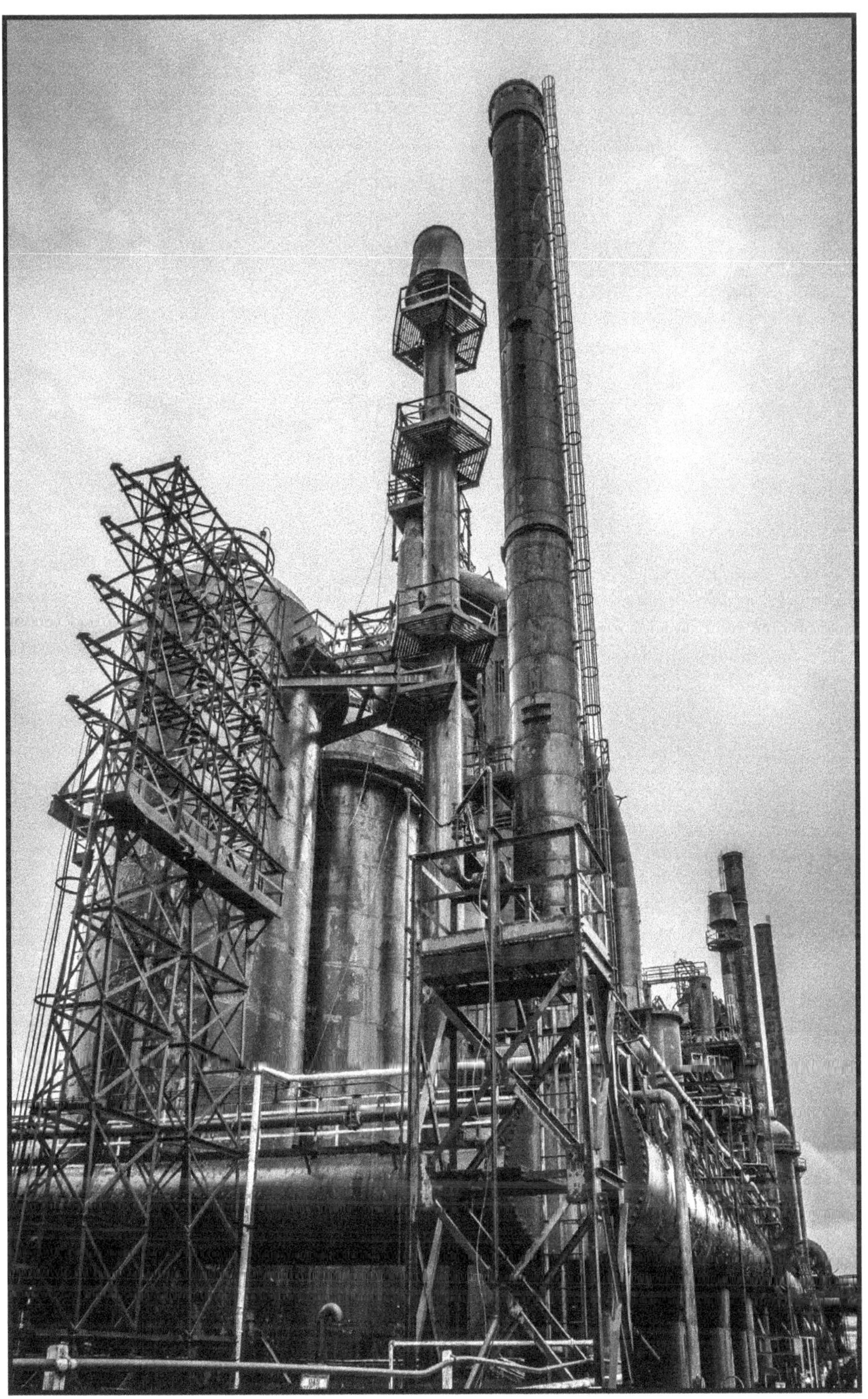

Divorce Papers

Steve Barichko

she said *i want to be done with you* and i said *no one wants*

to be done with me more than me which made her laugh

at the same courthouse that married us we signed

the dissolution and i asked that she leave me

at camp columbia *i'll figure out a way back don't worry*

in february the lush grass was long beige wheat and i lit

a slim cigar and stood still at the entrance the wheat opening

like a mouth and i wanted something predatory

to be lying in wait for me so that i could concede defeat

having seen it long after it had already seen me

Feral

Sophia Noulas

the Fox of Songi eats the monsters off maps saying
   one day I'll see pretty things,
while pale-tongues dart past reflected lamplight
  testing the heft of a voice's flavour

we played conservationists little boxes marked
help the leopards, save the cheetahs, for the tigers
parents pressing coins into their slots a la Genie
  miracles, we thought
   a proof of purpose

can you name me outside fences calling
  those that belong to nature like lady Lazarus and the fig wasps
do you remember the word for foliage after it is crusted under
  your weight sticking to your knees and elbows

people pour sugar on their dead tying garlic
  around their ankles to repel leeches but
meals are tasteless without season and
  needing no hands blood leaves

you wouldn't blame a twig
  snapping is what twigs do besides
discarded items are never wasted because
  something must feed the flowers

In Orbit

Fletch Fletcher

think *aphelion* and know
why he bundles in dark wool to sleep
the envy of dead
wandering the clothes-cluttered floor
besieging his bed
hiding treasures of coins and bills and cracked plastic
bottles that promised brightness and
barely brought the dim specter
of the moon's borrowed rays
as it too set somewhere in the floorboards and the trail
he left cooled to nothing and even if he could
be warm again it would entail so much
falling

House Hunters

Dan J. Vice

I'm looking for 5 acres in the heart of the heart
of the city center
close to restaurants and far from neighbors
a four-bed/three-bath with room for entertaining
an office & a studio space & walking distance to work
I like a Craftsman with curb appeal at a good price point
original hardwood, fireplace, sliding barn doors
& lots of character, but also
a midcentury-modern ranch-style bungalow
with clean lines
and a fenced-in backyard for the dogs
I need crown molding & an open concept
double vanities & subway tile backsplash & granite countertops—
no, quartz—and an island
two islands
I've been on this planet for 29 years and I'll be goddamned
if I go another day without shaker-style cabinets
This kitchen would have to be gutted
This bathroom would have to be gutted
I am an Automation Manager at a technology firm
that provides automation oversight for other automation
technology firms
My wife studies glassblowing
Our budget is $950,000

All the colours

Franziska Legg

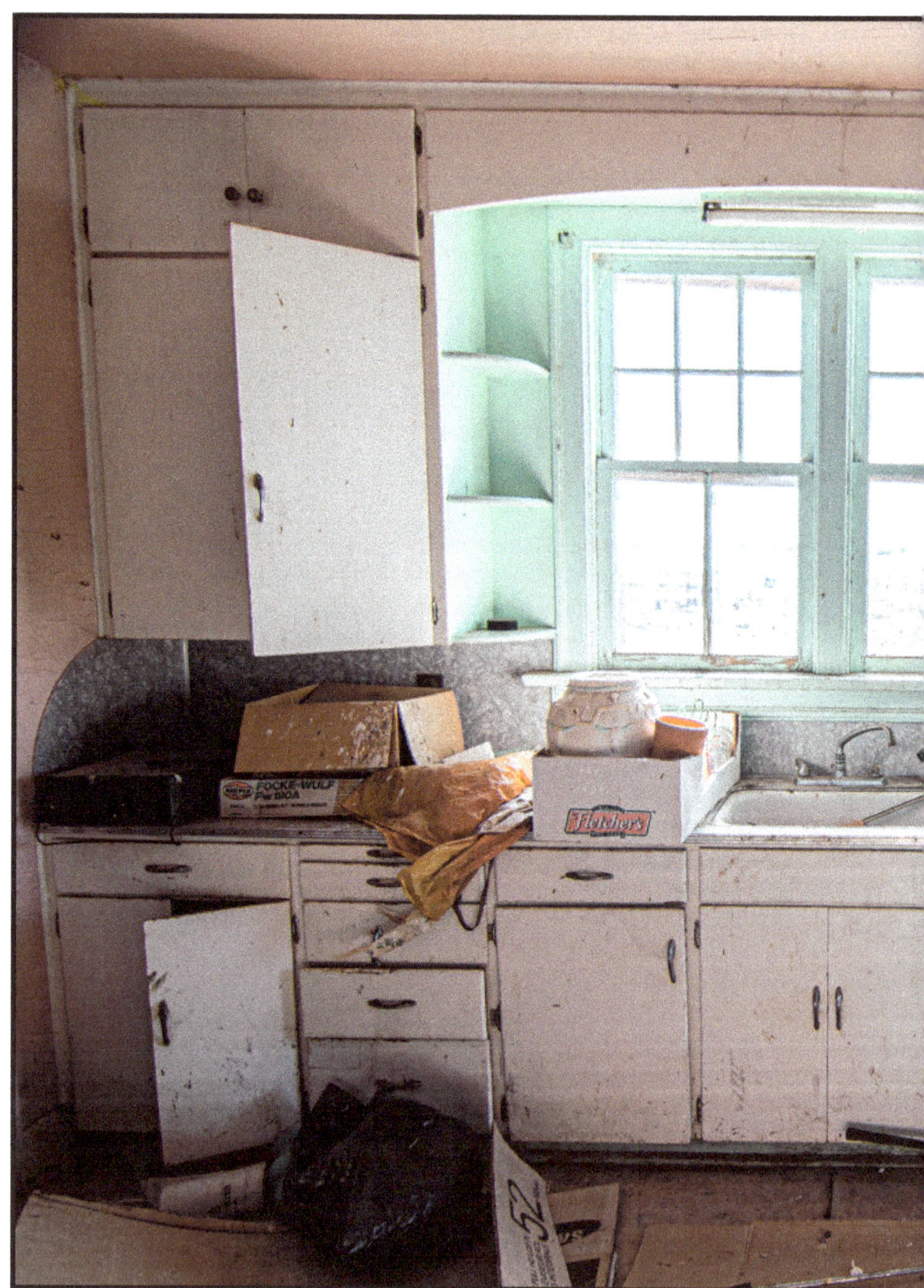

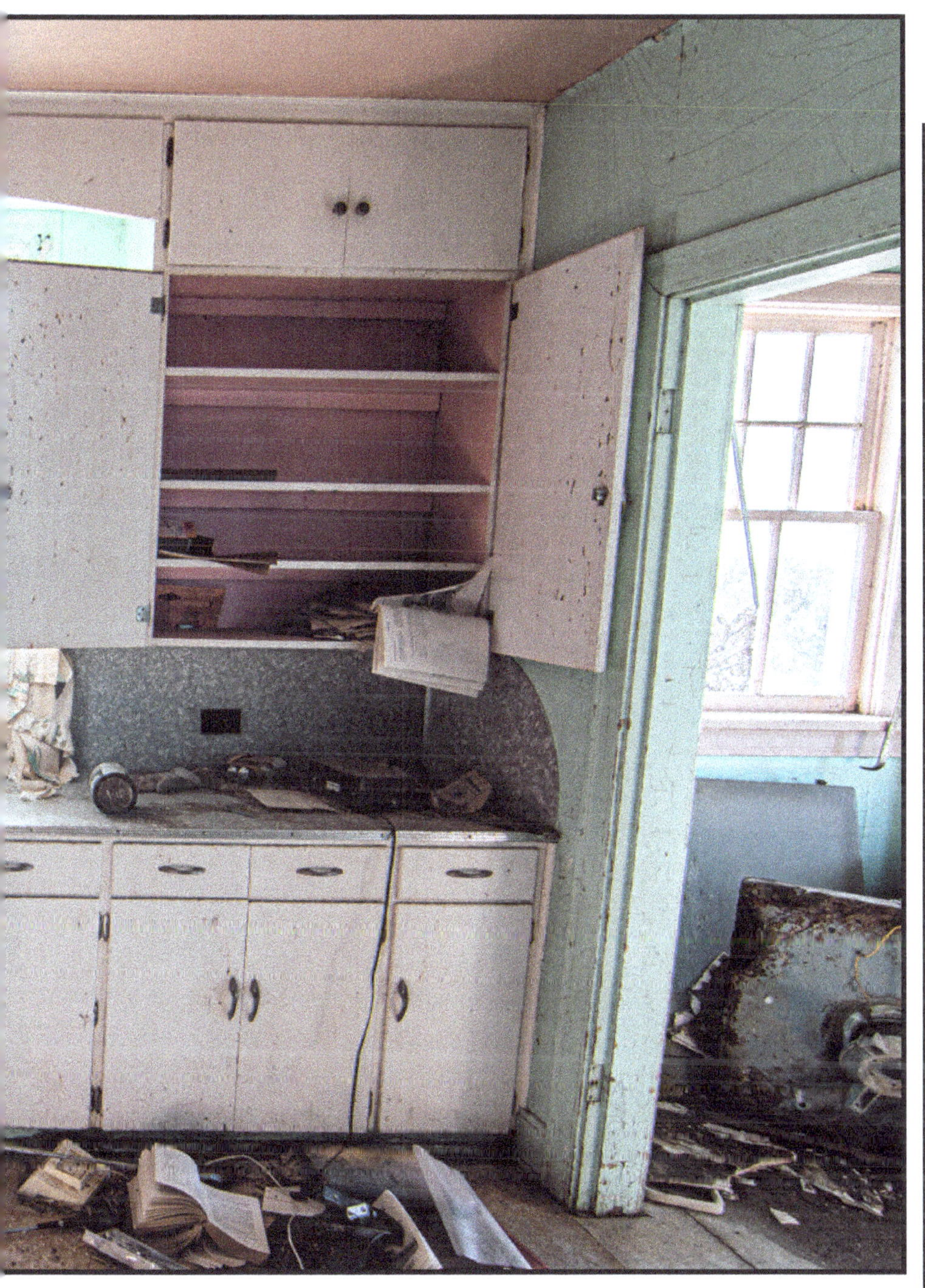

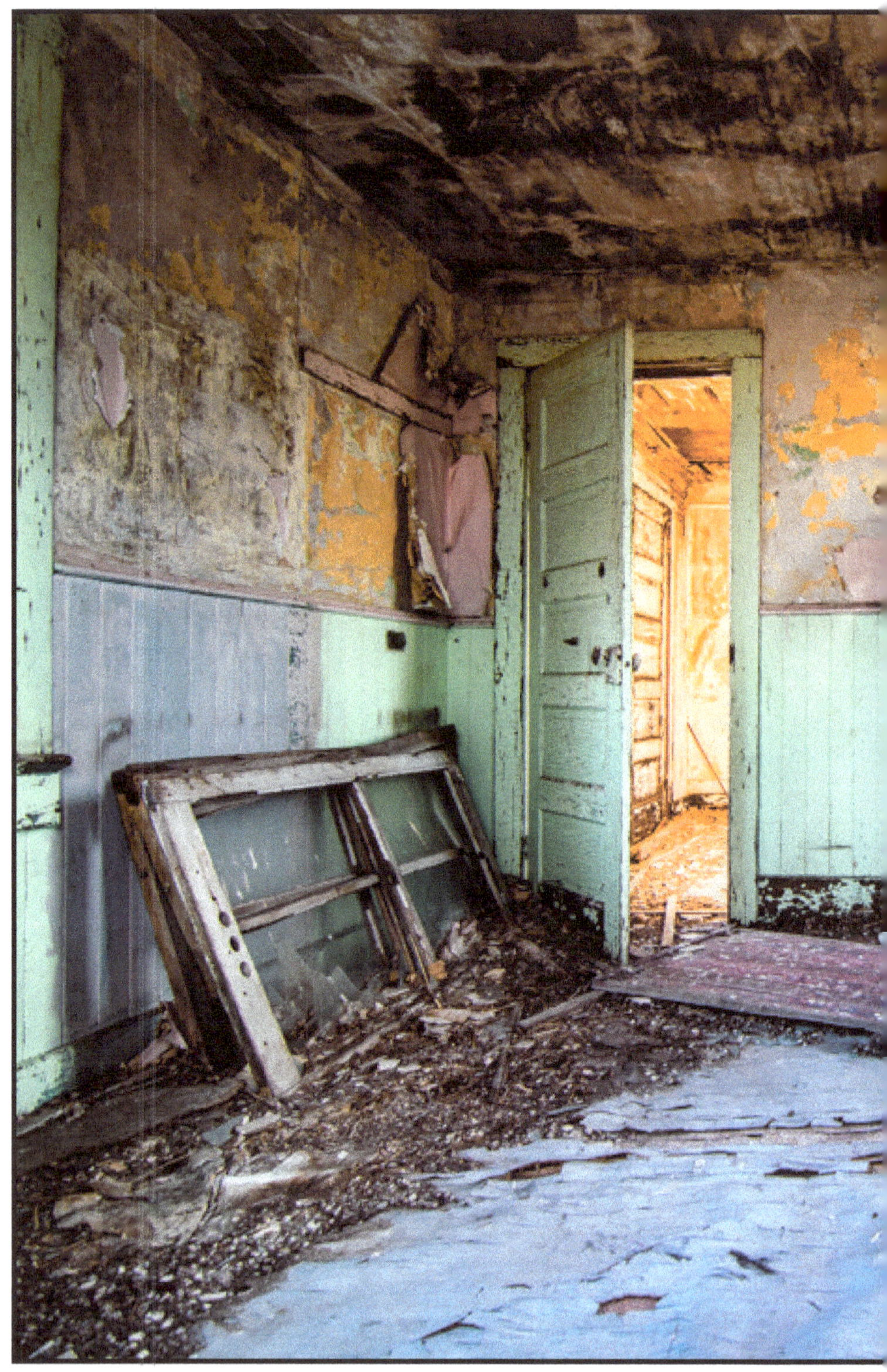

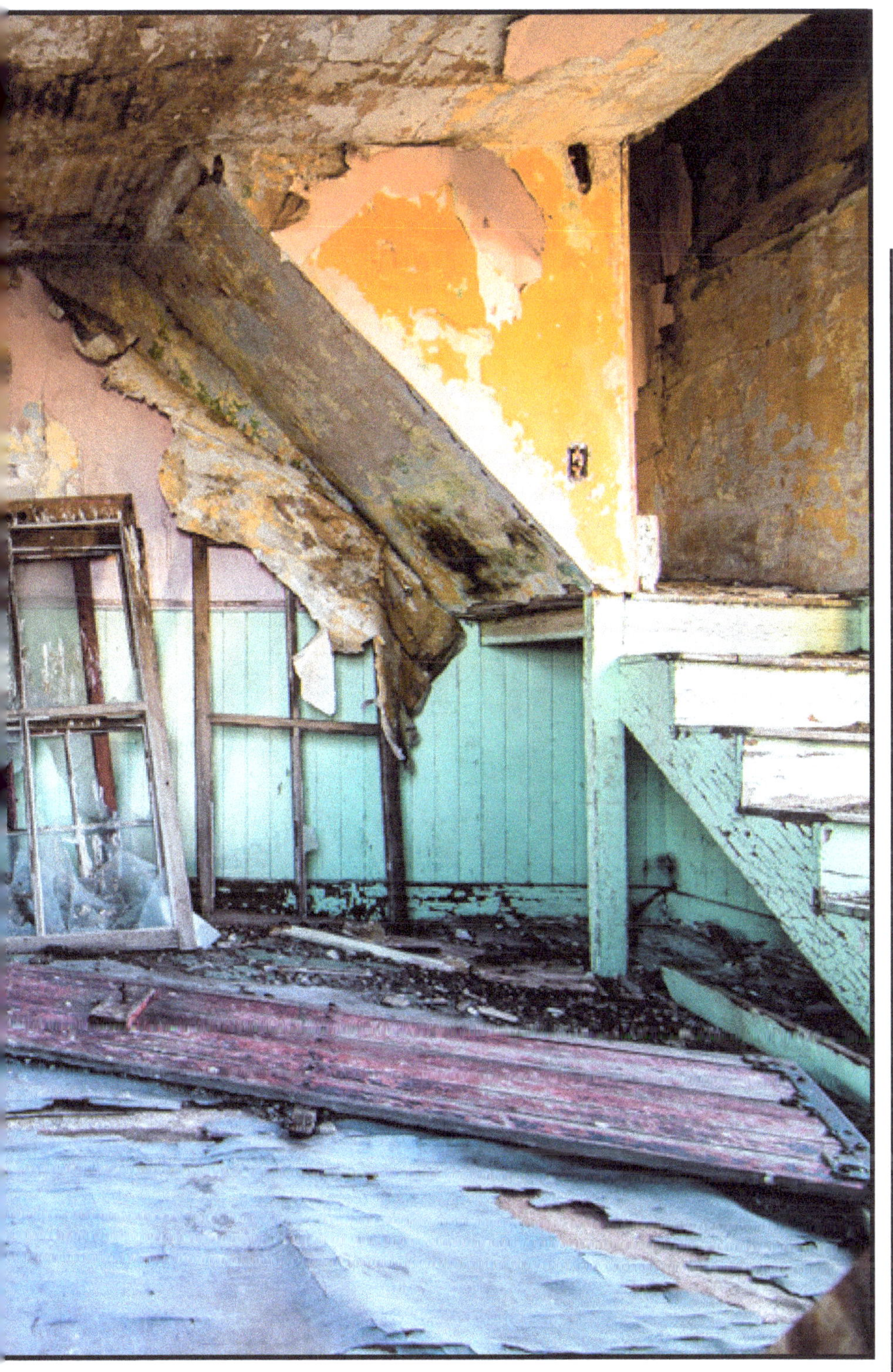

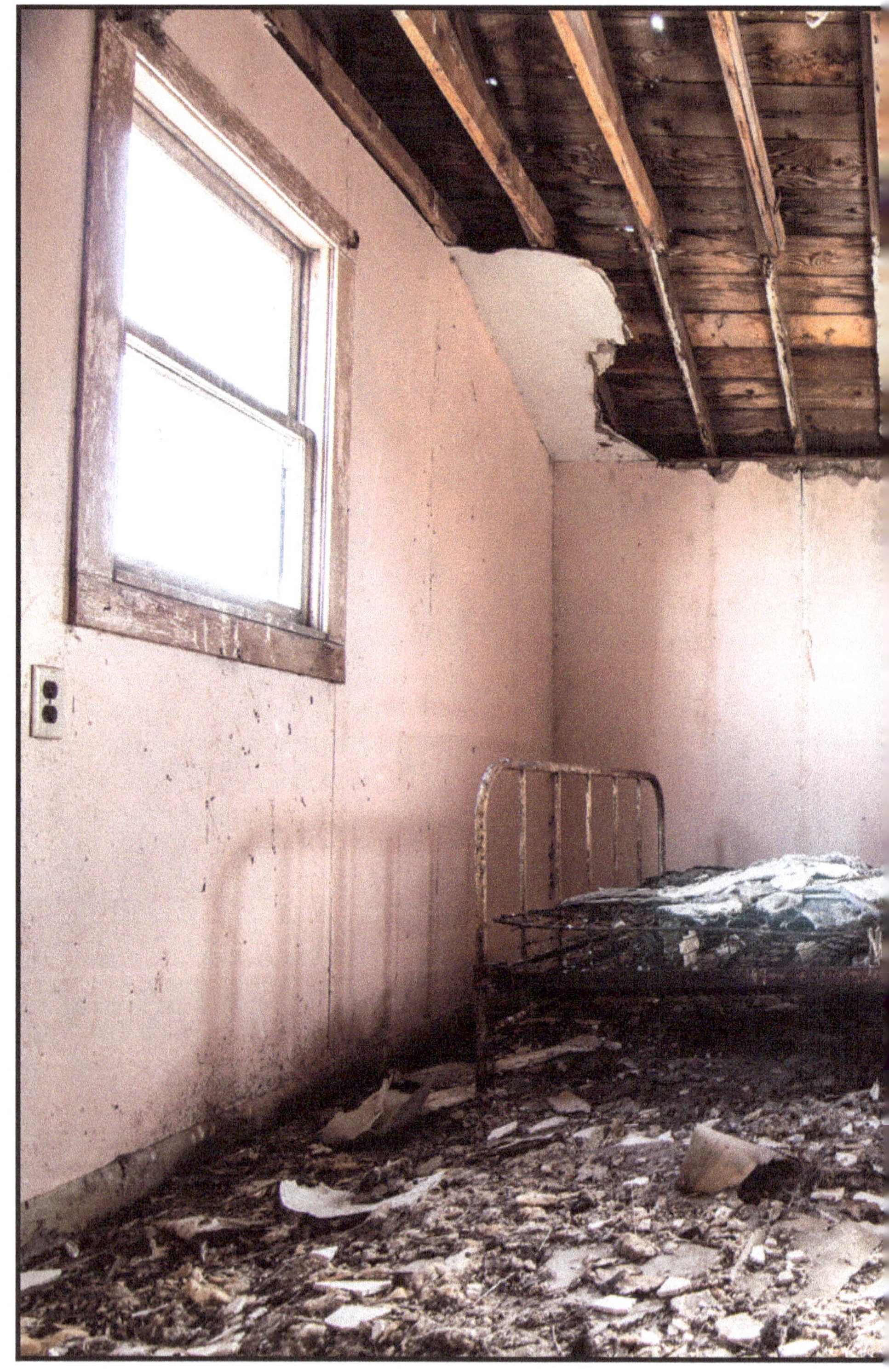

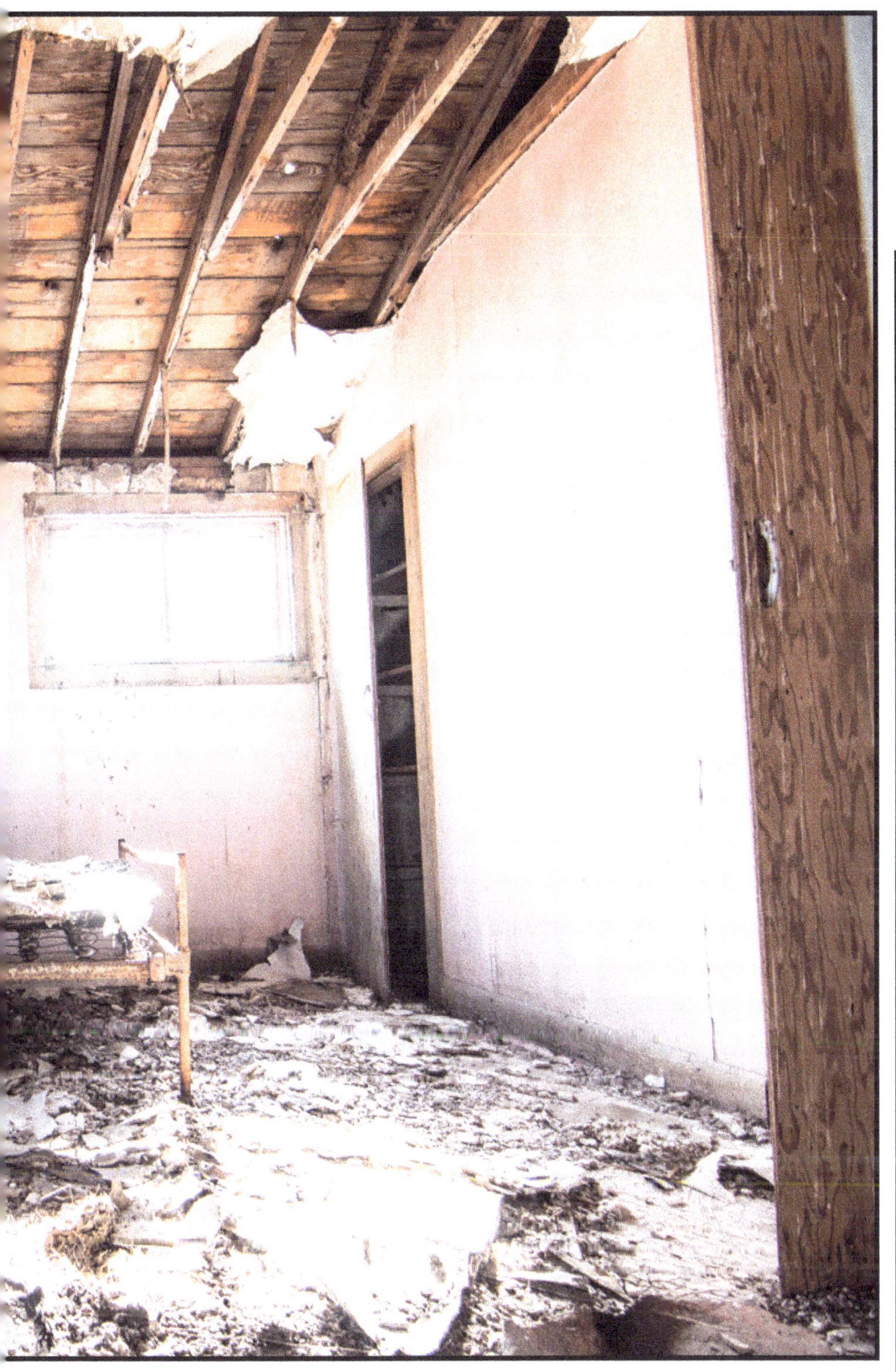

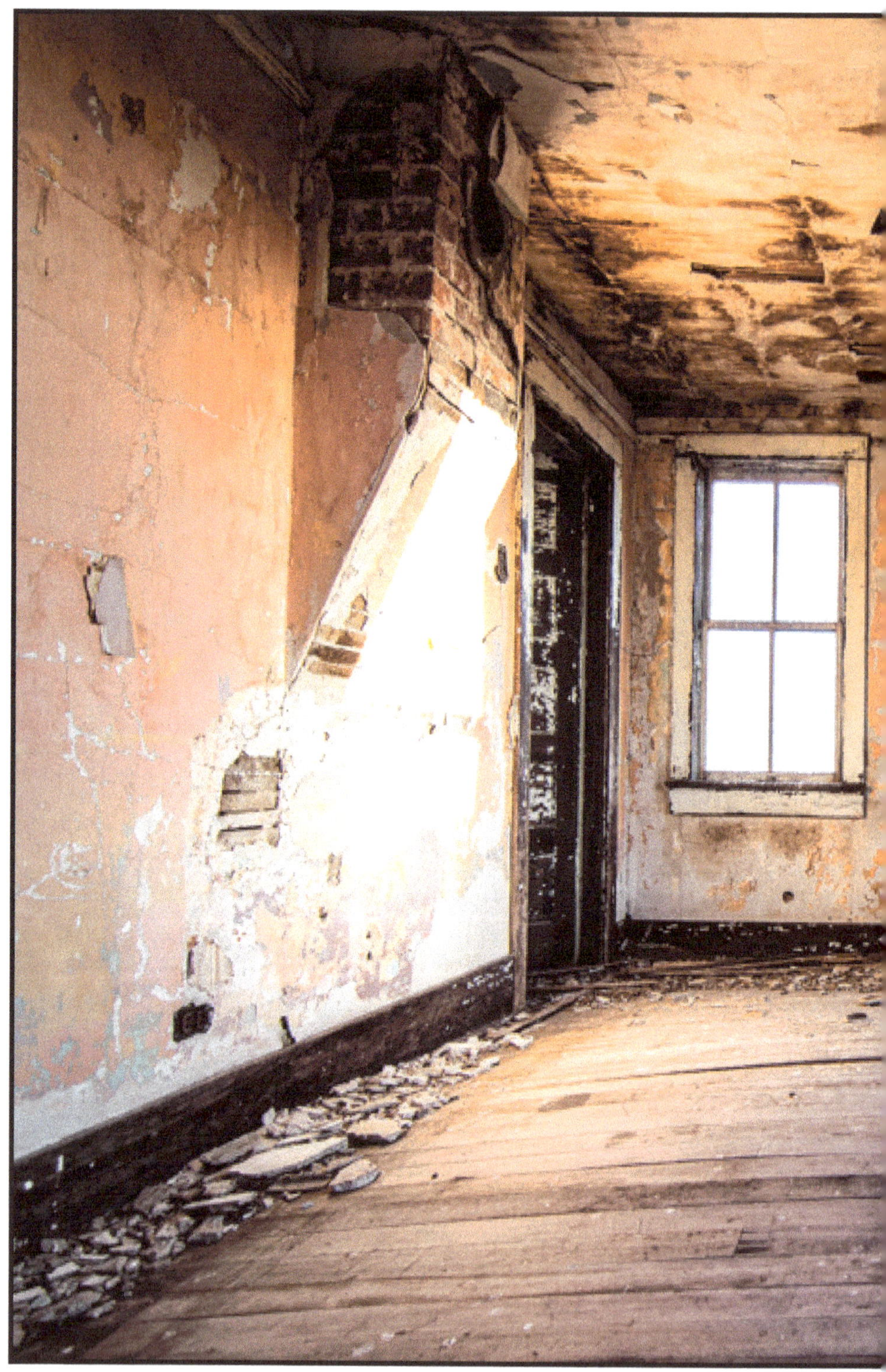

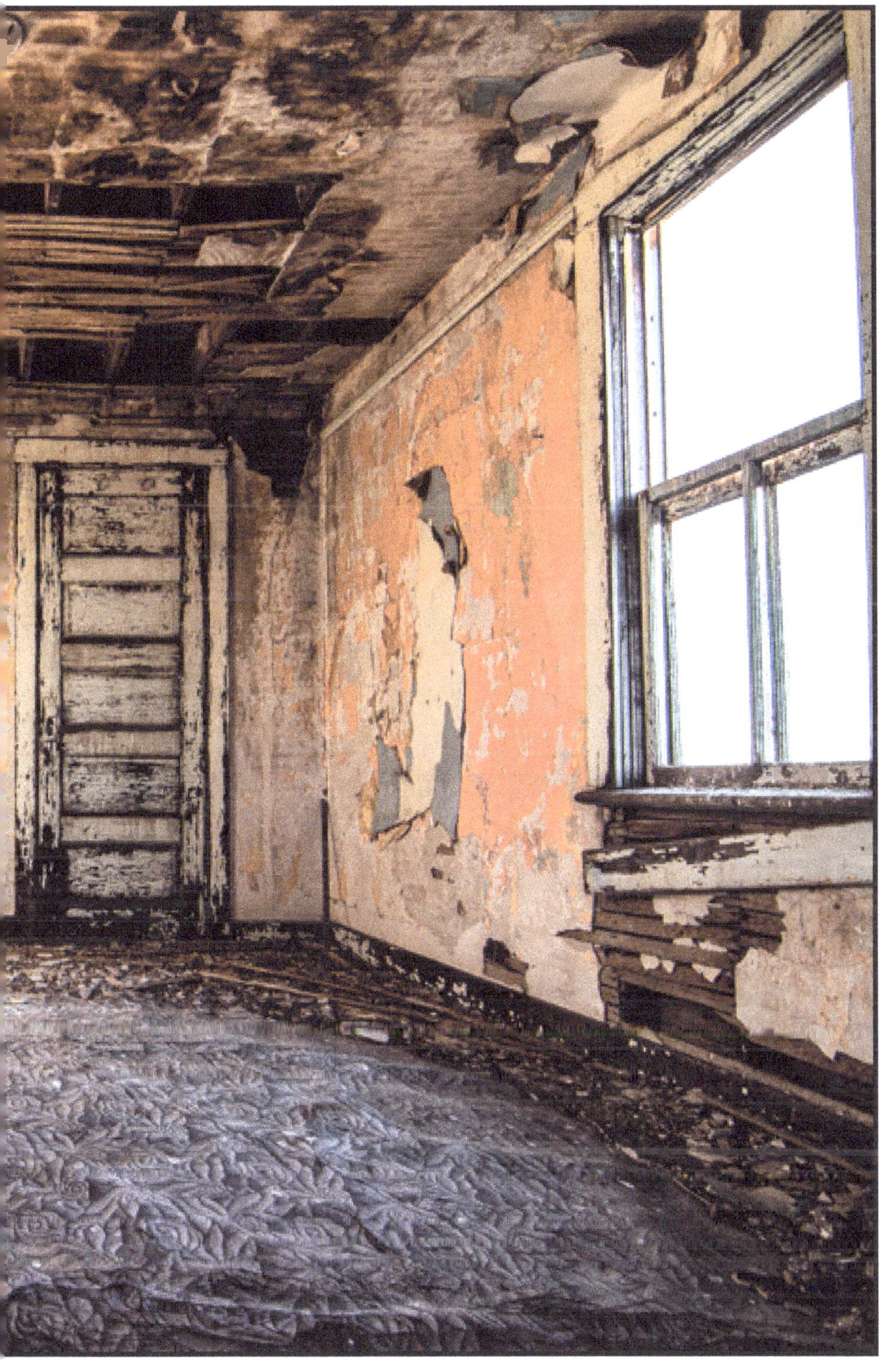

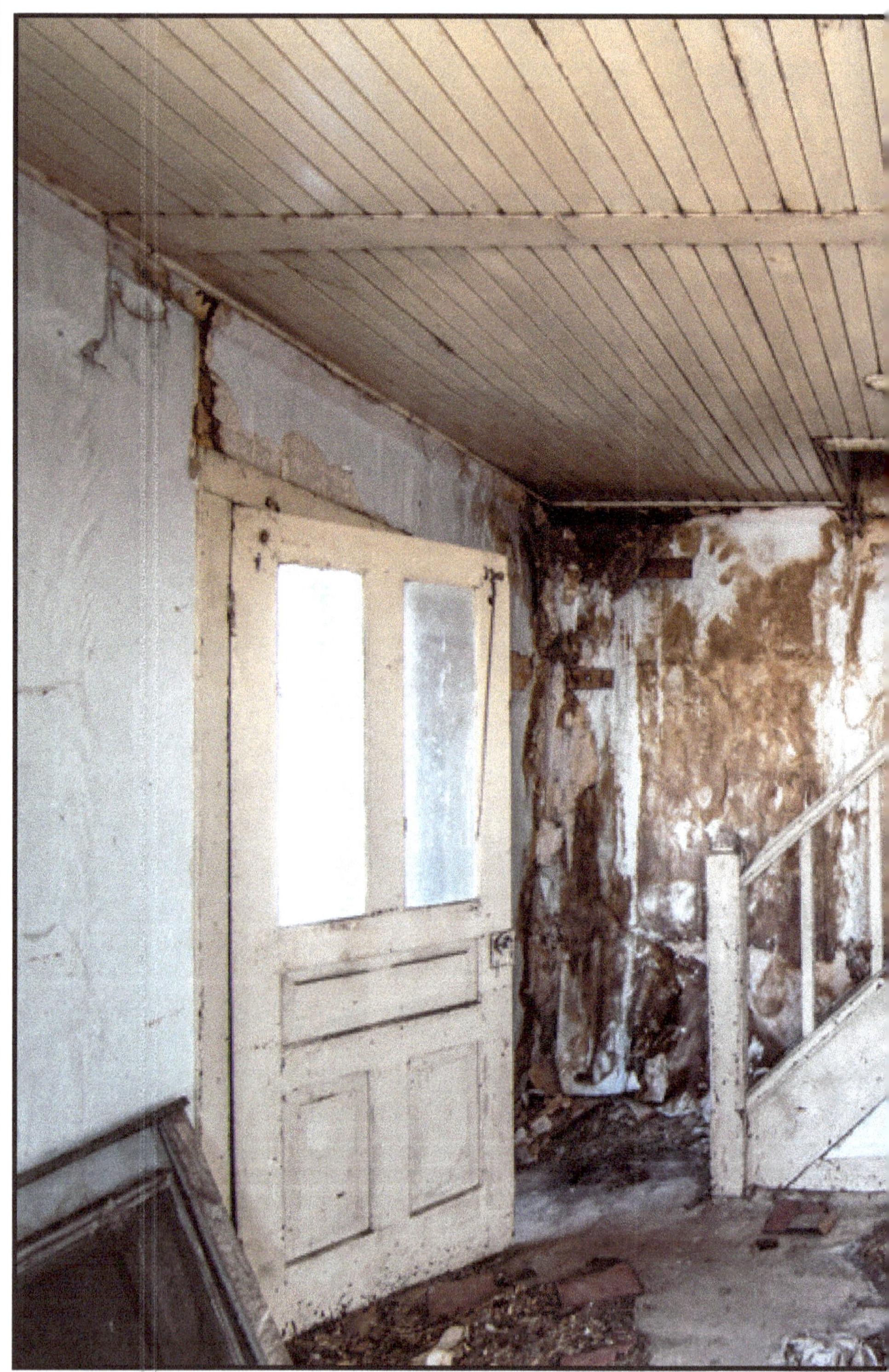

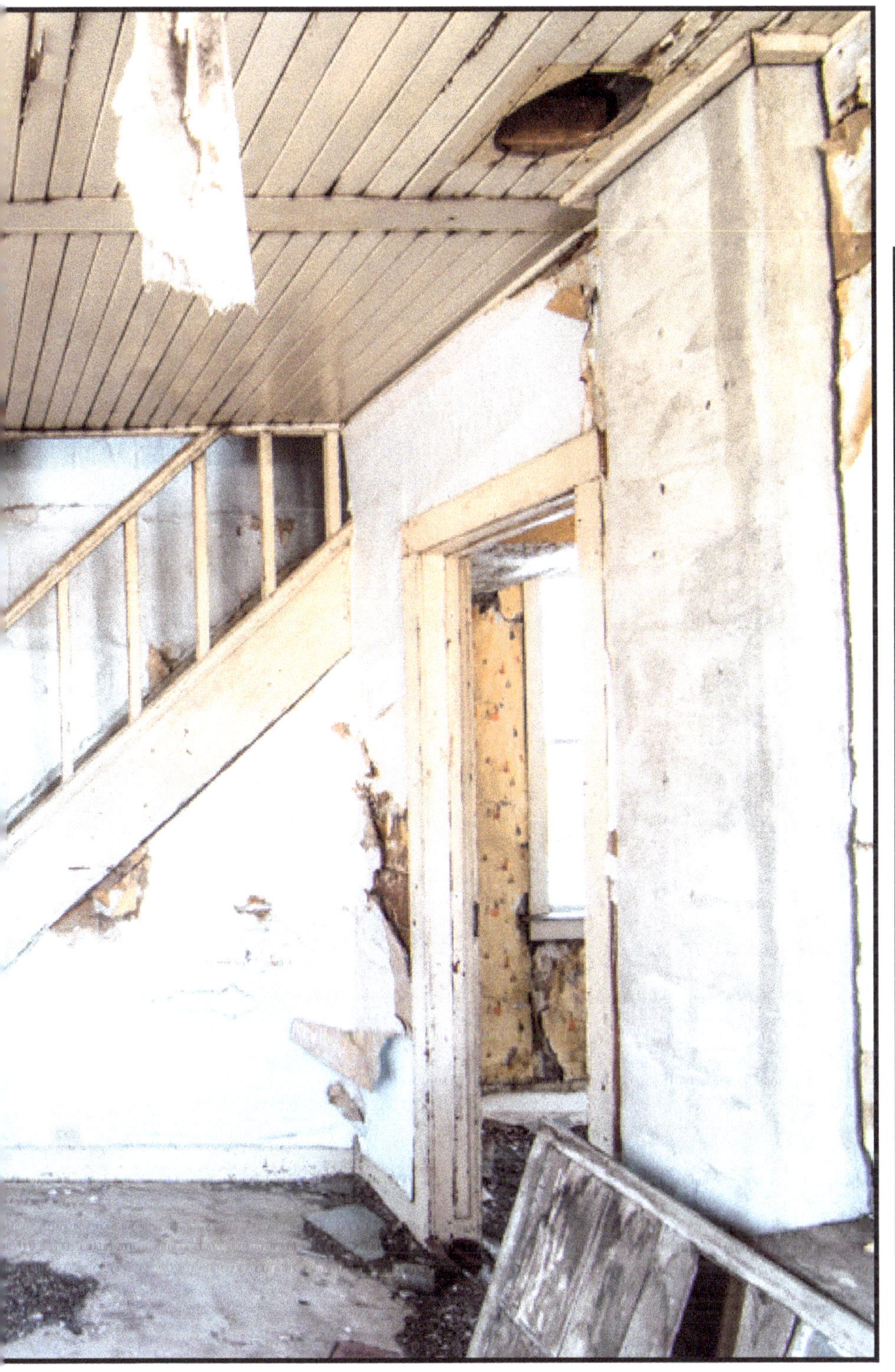

UNDISCOVERED COUNTRY

Leon Fedolfi

Auto heuristic fidgets –
flagella of sun across its surface.
I fall through, not down –
looking up at performance.
Light and pressure - now
white fading wall of weight.
It rises as I spindle deeper. Deep
into its brine and dark color.
What is hidden in this continent?
Where I cannot see, hear,
nor breathe, nor move.
No return.
It is not very different than the thought of it.
Surrounded by absence of thought,
bow of broken bone
and lungs filled with apocalypse.

Viral Age Advertising!

Steve Giliberto

Has anybody noticed how commercials on TV are trying to make the best of a very strange situation? So many of them lean toward the same track of showing how much they care and offering the old hang-in-there encouragement backed by regulation heart string plucking music. (Thank goodness piano players, violinists and harp players were declared essential workers.) The only thing certain in '...these uncertain times...' is the number of times ads will tell us how uncertain they are! But, fear not. Chik-Fil-A has assured us they will be ready and waiting to blow a hole in our aortas in person as soon as possible. And, post that delicious deep-fried orgy, we need to have no fears that we will be kept apart from our Cottonelle Mega Rolls any longer.

To be fair, it can't be easy trying to sell something to somebody who has been cooped up in their house for 8 weeks, is staring at you through Netflix auto-play glazed eyes, has a bowl of Cheetos in their lap, an orange stained remote control lying next to them and something stuck to their shirt that became unrecognizable several days before. Unless, that is, you are Frito Lay. We are way overdue for some new, edgy and exciting advertising. Something more appropriate for the times. Commercials that really embrace the moment. Ads for products that we can really wrap our emotionally mortar shelled heads around. Here is one that could finally pop us up from the face down mode on our couches into the upright position:

Greetings fellow homebound bunker hunkerers! Do the four walls seem closer than normal? Are you talking to plants not just because you heard its good for them but...because you're secretly hoping they'll answer back? Not to fear! The Blammo Streaming Network is here to let you in on brand new quirky, quixotic, quarantine streaming videos that will leaving you wondering why you haven't locked yourself in and thrown away the key sooner!

We've developed in our sterile filming studios housed in hermetically sealed, technologically advanced yurts spread out around beautiful Burbank, CA a whole new slate of binge-worthy programs to help turn nights into days and days into nights with ease. Here are some of our latest self-quarantine-help episodes you can have TODAY!

• 5 Easy Steps To Win An Argument With Yourself. Learn proven techniques on how to fight fair when you know how to push all your own buttons.

• Dance the blues away with our Dancing with the Household Appliance Stars series. Binge watch all episodes and be the first in your neighborhood to know how to get down and get funky with ALL your household appliances! Check out the latest episode: Waltzing With A Washing Machine. Learn how to let the machine take the lead!

• Introducing a new love interest to the family is always stressful, but now it has become almost impossible. Not to worry. A viewing of our new series, How to Introduce Your Blow-Up Doll Fiancé to the Whole Family takes the stress out having your new loved one meet your old ones. Subscribe right away and get the newly updated How-To-With-Zoom version!

Act right away and we'll send you an exclusive commemorative booklet written by a master of isolation, Hannibal Lector. Be the first to know how everything in quarantine can be made better with fava beans! Like everything else, supplies are limited! The booklet and the beans!

For as little as $9.99 a week, you will receive access to guaranteed never before seen ways to ride out home entombment and become the envy of neighbors who'll be asking, "Honey, come quick and look! What in the blue blazes are the people next door doing now?!"

You can physically distantly tell them how you're staying so well adjusted in lock down! By taking advantage of some of our newest groundbreaking releases, such as:

• Struggling with home exercise? Not anymore with our just added

episode on making exercise equipment with commonly found household items. Check out the latest: Gristle – Low Cost Exercise Bands!

• Cabin fever be damned after one viewing of Laundry Origami. Sock folding has never been this fun!

• Not to forget our valued LGBTQ customers, we've pushed isolation out and put romance back in to being homebound with our How To Have Your Mirror Reflection Become The One-Night Stand Of Your Dreams!'

• We have shows that are fun for the whole family, too! Everybody can enjoy, "You See Four Walls, We See An Endless Tic-Tac-Toe Board! Fill 'em up!

• The excitement just won't end when you and the whole houseful of fellow detainees learn how to go "Furniture Cushion Treasure Hunting!" Answer the age-old questions, "What the hell is that thing, how did it get in there and did it just blink at me??"

Blast away your boredom with Blammo! Why wait?!? Get your subscription NOW!

inside

Art by Sara DiDonato
Poetry by Emerson DeLaCamara

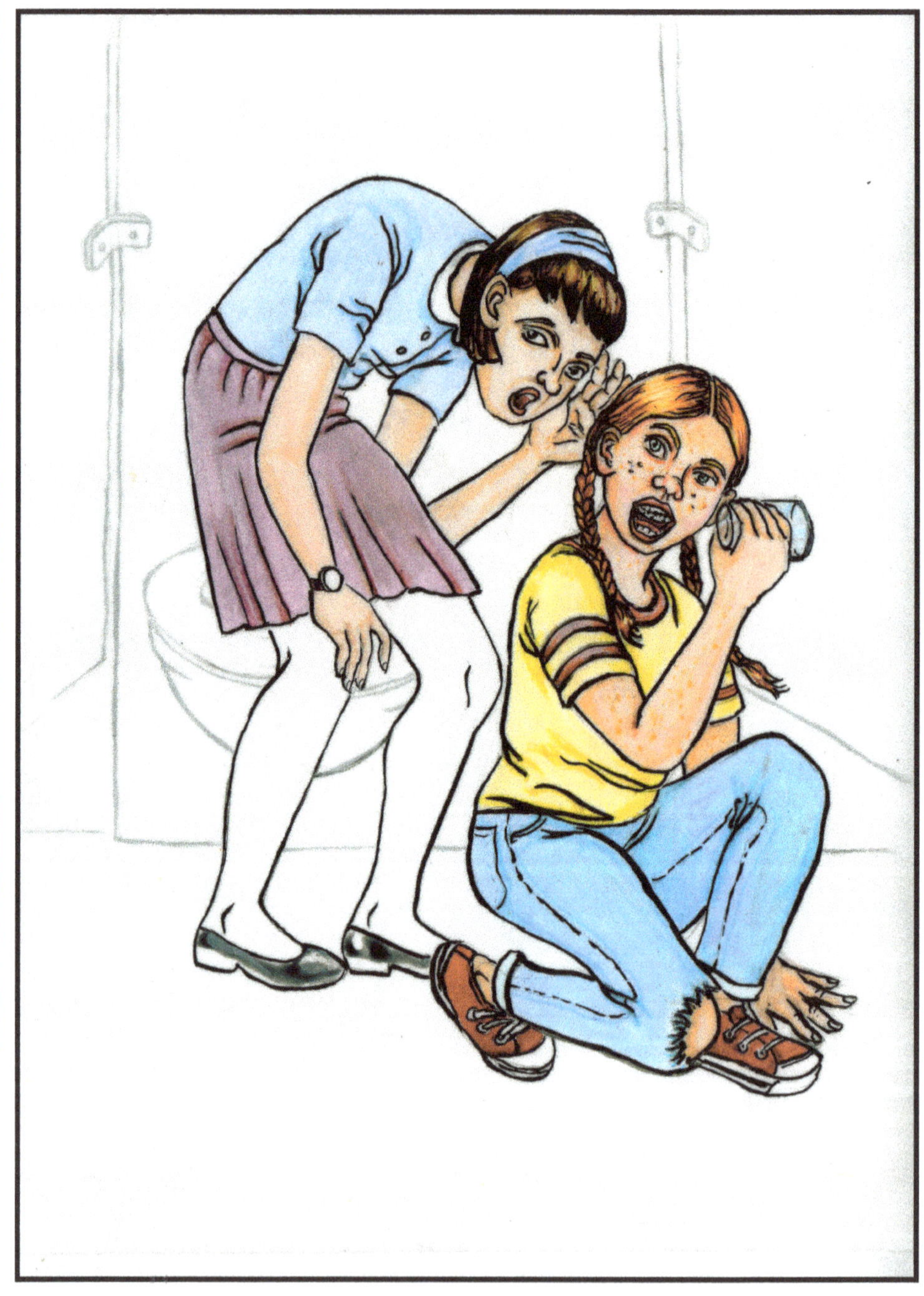

Whisper, whispering down the hall
The two girls watch for eyes
They're careful not to be caught at all
Under an indistinguishable guise

They stride past you and snicker
As they do to most
The wall between you just grows thicker
Friendship? A fading ghost

"Is that what she did?"
Crouching, hiding in the stall
"I heard it was him,"
They eavesdrop carefully through the wall

On the receiving end of the strafe
Every comment, so snide
No secret is safe
When they're on the inside

In Order Of Appearance:

Aidan White is a cartoonist and painter based in Great Barrington, Massachusetts.

Peter Engen grew up in the oldest Norwegian settlement west of the Mississippi as well as on the fly with his sometimes itinerant parents. He has lived most of his life in the hills and unglaciated valleys of Minnesota, Wisconsin, and Iowa. Some of his deepest poet yearnings were sought and quenched in the megalopolis cities of New York and Los Angeles before returning to his roots in the upper Midwest. He currently lives part-time on a solar-powered, green architecture farm near La Crosse Wisconsin.

Ishani Synghal is a first year MFAW candidate at the School of the Art Institute of Chicago. She is a poet first, but also writes creative non-fiction essays. Selected works are set to appear in the upcoming September 2020 issue of Levee Magazine. Ishani is based out of Chicago, San Francisco, and New York City.

Cierra Lowe is a poet and half-assed artist living in St. Louis, Missouri. She graduated from Webster University with a BA in philosophy, and her poems have been featured in Bad Jacket, Bellerive, and Sheila-Na-Gig. She published her first full-length collection of poetry and prose, The Horse and the Water, in 2017, and is currently working on her second as she pursues her BSN at UMSL. You can find new poems and other ramblings on her website, www.cierralovesyou.com.

Katie Hogan is a twenty year old emerging poet from Richmond, Virginia, pursuing a degree in creative writing as a second-year student at the University of Denver.

Raman Bhardwaj is a transplant freelance artist. He was born in India and has been living in Greensboro since 2018. He creates murals, canvas art, book illustrations, sometimes sculptures and multimedia works. He won a national award in India for illustrating a children book. He has also won Artpop Street gallery award 2019 in USA. He is a laidback guy who listens to Indian classical music and cooks chicken soup for his soul and is a homeopathy and Astrology enthusiast.

Sophie Hoss is a creative writing student at Stony Brook University on Long Island, New York.

Jasmine Ledesma can be found eating diamonds in New York. Her work has been published over twenty times including in places such as Into The Void and Vagabond City.

Haolun Xu is 24 years old and was born in Nanning, China. He immigrated to the United States in 1999. He was raised in central New Jersey and is currently studying Political Science and English at Rutgers University. Transitioning from a background in journalism and activism, he spends his time between writing poetry and the local seashore.

Michael Paramo is a Queer Xicanx artist-theorist and PhD Student at the University of British Columbia, located on the traditional, ancestral and stolen territory of the Musqueam, exploring themes of power, identity, and the metaphysical with a focus on portraiture. Born and raised on the traditional, ancestral, and stolen territories of the Tongva, Acjachemen, and Payómkawichum, Michael grew up in a Mexican-American family in the suburbs of north Orange County. Although they were conditioned from a young age to assimilate and adopt the values of settler colonial European American culture, they struggled to embrace and identify with its violent rigidity. One of their most difficult conflicts was accepting the settler colonial imposition that they were, or should become, a cisgender heterosexual man – a social construct which defined so much of their everyday life and suffocated their spirit's expression in the material realm. Michael has created art spontaneously since they were a child. They recall memories of their eagerness to share their newest creations with mother and artist Martha Guillen-Paramo. In their adolescence, Michael largely repressed their gift of artmaking as a result of their physical, mental, emotional, and spiritual challenges with existing. After several years of inconsistence and without institutional instruction, Michael created their first digital self-portrait in 2018, a medium which they continue to primarily work in. A year later, Michael began creating art under the artist name M.AZE, which is meant to reflect the critical role artmaking has played for them in navigating the internal and external labryinths of life survival amidst the unspeakable violence of the ongoing settler colonial project. In January 2020, Michael had their first public art showing at the University of British Columbia's second annual Art + Memory + Justice Symposium.

Vanessa Able is the author of the travel comedy Never Mind the Bullocks—a recipient of The Scotsman's Book of the Year Award—and founder and editor of the Spirit-Lit platform, The Dewdrop (www.thedewdrop.org). Vanessa is a freelance writer, previously published in the New York Times, National Geographic Traveler and Esquire Magazine. www.vanessaable.com

Felipe Echeverría-Gutierrez is an International Medical Graduate who obtained his Medical Doctor degree from San Francisco University in Quito, Ecuador. He describes his experience in Medical School as "The best time of his life. A period in my life in which I did not only grow as a physician and a person, but also gained invaluable friendships that persist up to this day". His last year of Medical School he completed his Undergraduate Medical Intern Year in Hospital Metropolitano, where he realized his passion and drive for Otolaryngology, specifically Otologic Surgery. Upon graduation, he decided to strive for an ENT residency in the United Stares of America, obtaining a 255 in Step 1, 254 in Step 2CK, first attempt PASS in Step 2CS and 242 in Step 3. He successfully completed a Clinical Observership at Johns Hopkins Bayview Medical Center, under the guidance of Dr. Matthew Kashima. He has applied for the 2020 Residency Match in both ENT and IM. He is currently preparing for Interview season. Felipe relishes socializing with family and friends. He also enjoys playing guitar (classical) and badminton on a weekly basis. Furthermore, he delights in writing free style poetry ('Ninfa de Ojos Aquosos' poem published in Prometheus Dreaming online magazine) and attending live music shows (both classical and contemporary styles).

Denise M Oehl was born and grew up in Ohio. She studied art at the The University of Toledo. She moved to NYC to continue her study at the School of Visual Arts where she received a Bachelor of Fine Arts with Honors in Painting. Oehl will most recently be exhibiting at The National Gallery in Gdansk, Poland in the Photography Museum. She has shown her work at John Davis In Hudson, NY, the Ely Center of Contemporary Art, in New Haven Connecticut, LABspace in Hillsdale, NY, WAAM, in Woodstock, NY and Pratt Institute, Brooklyn, NY and The Visual Studies Workshop in Rochester, NY. She currently resides and works in Hudson, NY.

Michael Hower is a photographer from the Harrisburg, PA area. His formal artistic education began in high school with courses at Lebanon Valley College and the Pennsylvania School of Art and Design. He moved on to study at Harrisburg Area Community College and Maryland Institute College of Art with focuses on painting, design and ceramics. Seven years ago, after picking up a digital camera for the first time, he fell in love with the medium, becoming self-taught. In photography Mike rediscovered a passion for art that he hadn't felt in years. His work focuses on historical themes, portraying human objects/structures in modified environments now devoid of human activity, particularly photographing places of abandonment with particular interest in industry, prisons and graffiti. His work conveys themes of wear, deterioration, and nature's reclamation of manmade environments via architecture and landscape. His works document the place-seeking journeys he has taken and showcase the process of learning and discovering our collective heritage. Michael's work has been featured in over one hundred and fifty shows and publications. Prominent juried shows include the Biggs Museum of Art and the Pennsylvania State Museum. Mike's work has also been selected for display at the Masur Museum of Art, Marshall University, the Banana Factory and the Maryland State House of Representatives. Recent publication credits include, Pennsylvania Magazine, Central PA

Magazine, The Santa Clara Review, and The Oakland Review of Carnegie Mellon University. Mike has also been selected for a number of solo and group shows including Abandoned Places, Rehoboth Art League, DE; Steelworks, Newark Arts Alliance, Newark, DE; Seekscapes, Art Association of Harrisburg, Harrisburg, PA; Foundations, WITF Public Media Center, Harrisburg, PA. His latest solo show Graffiti Scapes which ran from August to October 2019 at Penn College in Williamsport, featuring nearly 50 of his graffiti photographs and installations.

Steve Barichko is from Terryville, CT. His work has most recently appeared in Barren Magazine and Honey and Lime Lit, and is forthcoming in Doghouse Press. He lives in Terryville with his wife and daughter. He can be found @stevebarichko

Sophia Noulas is a graduate of Fordham University's Creative Writing Program. She volunteers as a reader for Electric Literature and she has connections to Frontier Poetry, the New York Poetry Society, and Fordham University's Unofficial Poetry Collective. She has been previously published in the Comma and Chaleur Magazine, and has upcoming work which will be published in La Piccioletta Barca. You can find her on Instagram @sophia_noulas

Fletch Fletcher is a science teacher, a poet, a brother, a friend, and an observer of how all people connect to everything around them. We need to strive for connection if we are to ever be better than we are.

Dan J. Vice shelters-in-place in Indianapolis with his wife, son, and two cats. He teaches writing and literature at the University of Indianapolis. He's really trying.

Franziska is an emerging photographer working in digital format. Her themes and subjects of study include: Southern Alberta landscape; Abandoned and decaying architecture (Rural and Urban); Abandoned and decaying vehicles. Born in Switzerland, she emigrated to Canada at a very young age with her parents and siblings. She began her journey with photography in her 20's. With this new art form she found freedom and individuality. She began a 365 photography project in 2014, which is still ongoing. She now resides in Lethbridge with her husband and three children.

Leon is an aspiring writer. He was awarded the 2020 Doug Draime Prize for Poetry sponsored by The Raw Art Review, and has published in Rumble Fish Quarterly, High Shelf Press and others. He has a book of poetry, The UnInvented Ear, coming out with UnCollected Press this fall.

Steve Giliberto is an essayist, a satirist, a critical observer of all things human. Giliberto's writing is driven by the constant absorption and regurgitation of the foibles of humanity's intersection with politics, society and popular culture. He seeks to share with readers his glimpses of humor and drama in each of them. They all smack of real truths. His writing is delivered in tones varying from the dark discomforting realities of our times to the humor of the absurd. By day he runs a technology consulting practice. By night he publishes his observations on his blog, https://oratoria.us. He holds a Certificate in Creative Non-Fiction Writing from the University of Washington.

Sara DiDonato was born in Naples, Italy, where her mother performed as a contortionist in a small traveling family circus. Sara received a BFA in Painting from the University of Iowa, and an MFA in Painting from the State University of New York at Albany. Her drawings and paintings have been exhibited in numerous solo and group exhibitions in national and regional venues, including the AAF Contemporary Art Fair (New York, NY); Center for the Arts Gallery, University at Buffalo; Rourke Art Museum (Morehead, MN); Albany Institute of History and Art (Albany, NY); and A.I.R. Gallery (Brooklyn, NY). Her work has been reproduced in New American Paintings and in the Stone Canoe journal. She is an Associate Professor at the State University of New York College at Brockport, where she teaches painting and drawing. She lives in Clarkson, NY with her partner, son, and three chickens.

Emerson DeLaCamara is an aspiring writer and photographer located in New England.

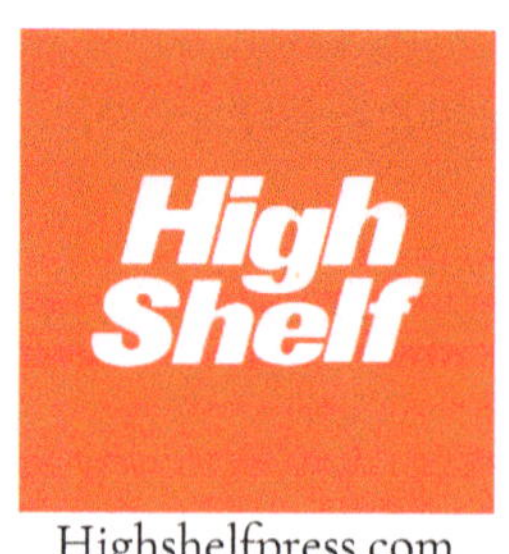

Highshelfpress.com